RULES FOR
COMPOSITORS AND
READERS

HART'S
RULES FOR COMPOSITORS AND READERS
AT THE
UNIVERSITY PRESS
OXFORD

Thirty-seventh edition
Completely revised

LONDON
OXFORD UNIVERSITY PRESS
NEW YORK   TORONTO

Oxford University Press, Ely House, London W. 1

GLASGOW NEW YORK TORONTO MELBOURNE WELLINGTON
CAPE TOWN SALISBURY IBADAN NAIROBI DAR ES SALAAM LUSAKA
ADDIS ABABA BOMBAY CALCUTTA MADRAS KARACHI LAHORE DACCA
KUALA LUMPUR SINGAPORE HONG KONG TOKYO

SBN 19 2129392

Originally compiled by Horace Hart, M.A.,
Printer to the University, 1883–1915. First
edition, 1893. Fifteenth edition (the first for
publication), 1904. Thirty-sixth edition,
1952. Thirty-seventh edition, completely
revised, 1967, and reprinted with additions
1970

PRINTED IN GREAT BRITAIN

PREFACE TO THE
THIRTY-SEVENTH EDITION

FOR this new edition, reset in a larger format, a complete review and, where necessary, revision of the contents has been made: the arrangement has been clarified, some obsolete material removed, new examples and rulings added, and the section on foreign languages enlarged.

Although the revision is the work of many hands, particular mention must be made of the assistance given by Mr. R. W. Burchfield, who gave valuable advice on lexical matters, and by Mr. J. S. G. Simmons, who contributed the new section on the setting of Russian.   V. R.

PREFACE

(1914)

IT is quite clearly set out on the title-page in previous editions of these Rules and Examples, that they were intended especially *for Compositors and Readers at the Clarendon Press*. Consequently it seems necessary to explain why an edition or impression is now offered to so much of the General Public as is interested in the technicalities of Typography, or wishes to be guided to a choice amidst alternative spellings.

On the production of the First Edition at the Oxford Press, copies were placed at the disposal of all Readers, Compositors, and Compositor-apprentices; and other copies found their way into the possession of Authors and Editors of books then in the printers' hands. Subsequently, friends of authors, and readers and compositors in other printing-offices, began to ask for copies, which were always supplied without charge. By and by applications for copies were received from persons who had no absolute claim to be supplied gratuitously; but, as many of such requests came from Officials of the King's Government at Home, in the Colonies, and in India, it was thought advisable, on the whole, to continue the practice of presentation.

Recently, however, it became known that copies of the booklet were *on sale* in London. A correspondent wrote that he had just bought a copy 'at the Stores'; and as it seems more than complaisant to provide gratuitously what may afterwards be sold for profit, there is no alternative but to publish this little book.

As to the origin and progress of the work, it was begun in 1864, when the compiler was a member of the London Association of Correctors of the Press. With the assistance of a small band of fellow members employed in the same printing-office as himself, a first list of examples was drawn up, to furnish a working basis.

Fate so ordained that, in course of years, the writer became in succession general manager of three London printing-houses. In each of these institutions additions were made to his selected list of words, which, in this way, gradually expanded—embodying what compositors term 'the Rule of the House'.

In 1883, as Controller of the Oxford Press, the compiler began afresh the work of adaptation; but pressure of other duties deferred its completion nearly ten years, for the first edition is dated 1893. Even at that date the book lacked the seal of final approval, being only part of a system of printing-office management.

In due course, Sir J. A. H. Murray and Dr. Henry Bradley, editors of the *Oxford Dictionary*, were kind enough to revise and approve all the English spellings. Bearing the stamp of their sanction, the booklet has an authority which it could not otherwise have claimed.

To subsequent editions the late Professor Robinson Ellis and Mr. H. Stuart Jones contributed two appendixes, containing instructions for the Division of Words in Latin and Greek; and the section on the German Language was revised by Dr. Karl Breul, Reader in Germanic in the University of Cambridge.

Recent issues of this work comprise many additions and some rearrangement. The compiler has encouraged the proof-readers of the University Press from time to time to keep memoranda of troublesome words in frequent—or indeed in occasional—use, not recorded in previous issues of the 'Rules', and to make notes of the mode of printing them which is decided on. As each edition of the book becomes exhausted such words are reconsidered, and in their approved form are incorporated into the pages of the forthcoming edition. The same remark applies to new words which appear unexpectedly, like new planets, and take their place in what Sir James Murray calls the 'World of Words'. Such instances as airman, airship, sabotage, seaplane, stepney-wheel, syndicalism, will occur to every newspaper reader.

Lastly, it ought to be added that in one or two cases a particular way of spelling a word or punctuating a sentence has been completely changed. This does not often mean that an error has been discovered in the 'Rules'; but rather that the fashion has altered, and that it is necessary to guide the compositor accordingly.   H. H.

CONTENTS

RULES FOR SETTING ENGLISH

These rules apply generally. They are
to be departed from only when authors
require their own spelling and punctuation to be strictly adhered to, or when
other exceptions are given in writing

RULES FOR SETTING ENGLISH

A OR AN

(a) Before all normal vowels and diphthongs: *an*

an actor	an exit	an oaf
an ailment	an iambic	an opening
an author	an instance	an uncle
an eagle		

(b) Before silent *h*: *an*

an heir	an honour	an hour

(pronounced exactly as if spelt eir, onour, etc.

(c) Before aspirated *h*: *a*

a harvest	a hero	a home
a height	a hill	a huge

Old usage supports:

an habitual	an heroic	an hypothesis
an heraldic	an historical	*also:*
an heretical	an hotel	an humble

where in all but the last example, the opening syllable is unaccented: 'an historical' but 'a history'. This is now old-fashioned. Use *a* in such cases unless it is necessary to follow a particular writer's individual style, in exact quotation, in printing diaries and letters, etc., where *an* is found in the original.

(d) Before a syllable beginning with a vowel but with the sound of *w*- or *y*-: *a*

a eulogy	a once-only	a unique
a ewe	a one	a useful

(*e*) Before all normal consonants: *a*

(*f*) With single letters and groups of letters *pronounced as letters*, be guided by pronunciation:

a B.B.C. broadcast   a K.L.M. flight
a C.M.S. missionary   a T.U.C. leader

but

an F.A. cup match   an O.U.P. book
an M.C.C. ruling   an R.A.C. rating

assuming that these will not be expanded by the reader and pronounced 'a Marylebone Cricket Club . . .', 'a Football Association . . .', 'a Royal Automobile Club . . .', etc.

If pronounced with a consonantal sound, however, initials must be preceded by *a*:

a NATO conference (pronounced 'Nato' not 'N.A.T.O.')

a MS. (normally pronounced 'manuscript' not 'em-ess')

ABBREVIATIONS AND CONTRACTIONS

As a general rule, abbreviations and contractions should be followed by a full point. However, full points may be omitted from shortened forms which occur with great frequency in a particular work. In addition, common abbreviations and contractions may appear, as directed, without points in display work.

When necessary, the names of days and months to be shown as below:

Sun. Mon. Tue. Wed. Thur. Fri. Sat.

Jan.	Feb.	Mar.	Apr.	May	June
July	Aug.	Sept.	Oct.	Nov.	Dec.

Where the name of a county is abbreviated, as Yorks., Cambs., Berks., Oxon., use a full point; but print Hants (no full point) because it is not a modern abbreviation.

4to, 8vo, 12mo, etc. (sizes of books), are symbols, and should not have full points. A parallel case is that of 1st, 2nd, 3rd, and so on.

In non-technical work print lb. and oz. for both sing. and pl.; not lbs. or ozs. Also omit the plural -s in the following: bu., cm., cwt., dwt., g. (= grammes), gr. (= grains), in., min., mm., sec. Insert the plural -s in hrs., qrs., yds. (In technical work BS. 1991 should be followed, see p. 53.)

Print £44. 1s. 4d., but £44 1s. 4d. in tabular matter. For decimal currency see p. 80.

When beginning a footnote, c. [*circa*], e.g., i.e., l. or ll., l.c., p. or pp., to be in lower case.

Print a.m., p.m. in lower case.

Generally print etc. *not* &c. Use the ampersand in names of firms, as Freeman, Hardy, & Willis. The ampersand may be used, as directed, in dictionary or similar work.

The points of the compass, N. S. E. W., when separately used, to have a full point: but print NE., NNW. These letters to be used only in geographical or similar matter: do not, even if N. is in the copy, use the abbreviation in ordinary composition; print 'Woodstock is eight miles north of Carfax.'

MS. = manuscript, MSS. = manuscripts, to be spelt out when used in a general sense. But in works in which the abbreviations are frequently used (such as Introductions, Commentaries, etc., dealing with classical texts and technical in character), and in references to particular manuscripts, the contracted forms should be printed; e.g. the Worcester MS., the Harleian MSS., Add. MS. 25642.

Print H.M.S. (His *or* Her Majesty's Ship); H.R.H.; I.W. (Isle of Wight); N.B.; PS. (not P.S.) for postscript or postscripts; Q.E.D.; R.S.V.P.; S.S. (steamship).

Print AS. (Anglo-Saxon), ME. (Middle English), OE. (Old English), OHG. (Old High German), and other similar combinations in philological works; but when an author prefers A.S., M.E., etc., no space should be put between the letters.

Print *O.E.D.* (*Oxford English Dictionary*), *D.N.B.* (*Dictionary of National Biography*), *C.O.D.* (*Concise Oxford Dictionary*), E.E.T.S., o.s./e.s. (Early English Text Society, Original Series/Extra Series), N.E.B. (New English Bible).

Mr., Mrs., Dr., etc., should be printed with a full point, but Mme and Mlle without.

For Saint use St. generally, but S. if this is the author's consistent preference; both with full point (plural SS.). Before a French name use S. (masc., with point) or Ste (fem., no point).

Print Bt. for Baronet; Kt. for Knight; Revd. (*not* Rev.) for Reverend.

Omit the apostrophe in the plurals B.Litt.s, M.A.s, M.P.s, Q.C.s, the sixties, the 1960s.

Print Anzac, Aslib, Derv, Fiat, GATT, Naafi, NAAFI, NALGO, Nato, NATO, Octu, OCTU, SoGAT, Unesco, UNESCO, and any similar formation *which is commonly pronounced as a single word*, in accordance with what appears in the copy. The initials of the name of any organization, etc., *not normally pronounced as a single word* should be printed in capitals with points, as O.E.E.C., P.A.Y.E., S.P.C.K., T.U.C., W.E.A., W.H.O.

Print A-bomb, H-bomb (no points).

Print U.N. (= United Nations), *not* UN or U.N.O. or UNO.

Print ITV, TV (no points).

Print C. (Celsius or centigrade), F. (Fahrenheit), but without points in scientific work.

As a rule, print nineteenth century, *not* 19th cent.; 9 per cent, *not* 9%.

For Fig., No., Pl. see p. 11.

ABBREVIATIONS USED IN THE METRIC
SYSTEM OF WEIGHTS AND MEASURES

IN printing English scientific works[1] (or any other work in which these abbreviations are used with great frequency) use the following abbreviations for metric units both in singular and plural form:

Metre

km	kilometre	m^2	square metre
m	metre	cm^2	square centimetre
cm	centimetre	mm^2	square millimetre
mm	millimetre	m^3	cubic metre
		cm^3	cubic centimetre
		mm^3	cubic millimetre

Gramme		*Litre*	
kg	kilogramme	l	litre
g	gramme	dl	decilitre
mg	milligramme	ml	millilitre (mil)*
		dml	decimil*
		cml	centimil*

* In order to express conveniently the smallest doses prescribed, the Board of Trade authorizes the use of the term *mil* (for the millilitre) and of the two subdivisions of this measure—the decimil and the centimil.

When larger multiples or smaller submultiples of metric units are needed the range is extended by prefixing the abbreviations:

T: tera	×	1 000 000 000 000
G: giga	×	1 000 000 000
M: mega	×	1 000 000
k: kilo	×	1000

[1] For the corresponding abbreviations in French see pp. 83–4. The abbreviations used in medical works vary in some particulars from the above list.

d: deci	$\div$		10
c: centi	$\div$		100
m: milli	$\div$		1000
μ: micro	$\div$		1 000 000
n: nano	$\div$		1 000 000 000
p: pico	$\div$	1 000 000 000 000	

e.g. 1 μm = 1 micrometre

$\qquad$ = 1 millionth of a metre

(sometimes called a micron).

BOOKS OF THE BIBLE

NAMES of the books of the Bible should be abbreviated as follows:

Old Testament

Gen.	1 Kgs.	Eccles.	Obad.
Exod.	2 Kgs.	S. of S.	Jonah
Lev.	1 Chr.	Isa.	Mic.
Num.	2 Chr.	Jer.	Nahum
Deut.	Ezra	Lam.	Hab.
Josh.	Neh.	Ezek.	Zeph.
Judg.	Esther	Dan.	Hag.
Ruth	Job	Hos.	Zech.
1 Sam.	Ps. (*pl.* Pss.)	Joel	Mal.
2 Sam.	Prov.	Amos	

New Testament

Matt.	2 Cor.	1 Tim.	2 Pet.
Mark	Gal.	2 Tim.	1 John
Luke	Eph.	Titus	2 John
John	Phil.	Philem.	3 John
Acts	Col.	Heb.	Jude
Rom.	1 Thess.	Jas.	Rev.
1 Cor.	2 Thess.	1 Pet.	

Apocrypha

1 Esd.	Wisd.	Bel & Dr.
2 Esd.	Ecclus. [= Sir.]	Pr. of Man.
Tobit	Baruch	1 Macc.
Judith	S. of III Ch.	2 Macc.
Rest of Esth.	Sus.	

There are also the extra-short forms Gn., Ex., Lv., Nu., Dt., etc. (O.T.), and Mt., Mk., Lk., Jn. (N.T.)—legitimate in narrow measure or marginal references.

CAPITALS, SMALL CAPITALS, AND LOWER-CASE INITIALS

CAPITAL AND LOWER CASE

CAPITAL letters should be used for proper names: Smith is a baker; Baker is a smith.

They should be used also **for:**

(*a*) Prefixes and titles forming part of a compound name:

Sir Roger Tichborne, the Bishop of Oxford, the Duke of Wellington. [Note: in historical writing lower case is sometimes used, e.g. the duke of Normandy, the earl of Arundel. This should not be followed unless definitely prescribed as the style of the work or series.]

The King of England, the Prince of Wales— when the title of a particular person; but in a general sense lower case is correct: 'every king of England from William I to Richard II'; for 'king' is used here in a perfectly general sense, where 'monarch' or 'sovereign' would be equally correct.

(*b*) Parts of recognized geographical names:

Northern Ireland, i.e. the six counties, a political division; but 'northern England', a plain description in general terms. Similarly Western Australia, West Germany (officially the Federal Republic), East Germany (officially the German Democratic Republic), etc. Also New England (a recognized, though not political, division of U.S.A.); contrast 'a new England beyond the seas', which could be anywhere.

Firth of Clyde, Norfolk Broads, Straits of Gibraltar, Plymouth Sound, Thames Estuary (but estuary of the Thames).

Also River Plate (Río de la Plata), East River (New York), but the Thames, or the river Thames.

Topographical and urban names: planting wheat in the Fifty Acre, Trafalgar Square, Addison's Walk, London Road (if official name), but 'the London road' (that leading to London).

(*c*) Proper names of periods of time or natural phenomena, historical eras and events:

Palaeozoic, Carboniferous, Tertiary, Palaeolithic period, Neolithic period, Old (New) Stone Age, Bronze Age, Iron Age. Also such terms as Chalcolithic, Early Minoan, Beaker Folk, etc., if these have a definite archaeological significance, as shown by author's consistent usage.

Antiquity (occasionally used for Greek and Roman history), Classical, Byzantine, Dark Ages, Middle Ages, Renaissance (dark ages, middle ages, renaissance would be too general, but medieval (lower case) is accepted as referring specifically to the Middle Ages).

First World War, Second World War, etc., or World War I, II, if the copy is consistent.

(*d*) Proper names of institutions, movements, etc.:

Those derived from personal names or titles— Christianity, Marxism, Buddhism; and those not so derived—Islam, the Church (when a proper name of the Christian Church as a whole, or of any institution called Church, e.g. (Roman) Catholic Church, Church of England; but lower case for the building, and for a church in a general sense, e.g. any church or sect).[1]

---

[1] In the New Testament, 'church' (*ekklesia*, otherwise translated 'congregation' or 'assembly') has lower case, as not yet a formal title.

Church and State—both capitalized when viewed as comparable institutions, also 'the State' traditionally in political philosophy; the Crown, Parliament, Congress (U.S.), House of Commons (of Representatives, U.S.), House of Lords, Senate (when officially so called, but 'the House of Lords should be a senate composed of elder statesmen'), Treasury (British and U.S.), Ministry of Finance, etc.

H.M. Government, or the Government, in official parlance and meaning a particular body of persons, the Ministers of the Crown and their staffs; but the government (lower case) is correct in general senses.

(e) Parties, denominations, and organizations, and their members:

Conservative, Labour, Liberal (in British politics); Socialist, Social Democrat, Christian Democrat (European countries, etc.); Republican, Democratic (U.S.A.); and so on. (But liberal, socialist, republican, democratic, etc., as normal adjectives when not party titles.)

Baptist, Congregationalist, Methodist, Presbyterian, Unitarian, Church of England, Anglican, Roman Catholic, Orthodox (i.e. Eastern Orthodox), Reformed, Evangelical (continental and U.S.). (But congregational (singing, polity), reformed, unitarian views of God, orthodox belief, catholic sympathies in non-denominational sense.)[1]

Reformed, Puritan, etc., may be capitalized by particular authors or in particular contexts to make specific reference to the Reformation (sixteenth–seventeenth centuries—Europe) or Puritanism, as

---

[1] Note that the Church of Scotland is (since 1690) presbyterian in government, but the Church of England is episcopal; there exist also the Episcopal Church in Scotland and the Presbyterian Church of England. Only the *capitalized* terms are official titles: there are no such bodies as the Presbyterian Church of Scotland or the Episcopal Church of England.

against reforming and puritan tendencies elsewhere, e.g. in monastic orders, non-Christian religions, etc.

The general rule is: capitalization makes a word more specific and limited in its reference: contrast a Christian scientist (man of science) and a Christian Scientist (member of the Church of Christ Scientist).

(*f*) Titles of office-holders:

In certain cases and certain contexts these are virtually proper names of persons: H.M. the Queen, the Prime Minister, the Archbishop of Canterbury. The extension of this principle depends on the context: the President, e.g. of U.S.A., of Magdalen College, Oxford, etc.

Similarly, the Bishop of Oxford, the Dean of Christ Church; and within a particular diocese, the Bishop, or particular cathedral or college, the Dean (referring to a particular individual, or at least holder of a particular office: the Bishop is *ex officio* chairman of many committees). (But: when he became bishop, the bishops of the Church of England, appointment of bishops—such cases are better printed in lower case, and so with other office-holders.)

(*g*) Names of ships, aircraft types, railway engines, trade names, etc.:

The *Cutty Sark*, H.M.S. *Dreadnought* (italic for ships' names, see also p. 23); the Königs, the fastest German battleships in 1916 (capitals but not italic for *types* of ships).

The Spitfire, the Flying Fortress, the Dakotas of the 1939–45 war. These are types, since aircraft do not usually have individual names; but 'the U.S. bomber Enola Gay which dropped the atom bomb over Hiroshima on 8 August 1945' (not italic as not official like a ship's name).

A Viscount, an Elizabethan, a Concorde (airliners).

A Ford Cortina, a Hillman Imp (trade names).

Aspro, Cow & Gate, Dreft, Persil, Tide, etc. Capitals must be used for proprietary names, which would sometimes be absurd with lower case, e.g. 'Mrs. Jones washed with tide.'

Figure, Number, Plate (Fig., No., Pl.), should each begin with a capital, unless special instructions are given to the contrary.

Pronouns referring to the Deity should begin with capitals only if so requested by the author: He, Him, His, Me, Mine, My, Thee, Thine, Thou; but even so print: who, whom, and whose. If the copy is not consistent or the author not insistent, lower case for all pronouns is much to be preferred, and as this has the authority of the Bible and the Book of Common Prayer there is no real justification for capitals *as a rule*. They are now either old-fashioned or a personal preference of some (especially devotional) writers. (The Church of Scotland requires capitals in all its official publications.)

Adjectives derived from proper names

(i) To be capitalized, from usage, or when connection with the proper name is still felt to be alive:

Christian, Dantesque, Hellenic, Homeric, Machiavellian, Platonic (historical and philosophical), Roman (Catholic, etc.); but machiavellian (intrigue, etc.), platonic (love), roman (type).

(ii) Not to be capitalized when connection with the proper name is remote:

french (chalk, cricket, polish, etc.), herculean (= mighty, gigantic), lilliputian, morocco (leather) (cf. suede (leather: originally = Swedish)), pharisaical, quixotic, roman (figures, etc.) (cf. arabic, italic), titanic.

Verbs and other words derived from proper names

(i) To be capitalized:

Christianize, Hellenize, Latinize, Romanize (in historical and cultural senses).

(ii) Not to be capitalized:

The more common words derived from proper names, as ampere, bowdlerize, boycott, doily, hansom cab, holland, inverness, japan (black lacquer), jersey (garment), latinity, macadamize, mackintosh, may (blossom), ohm, pasteurize, philippics, quisling, russia leather, sandwich, ulster, volt, watt, wellington (boot). Likewise the names of metres: alcaics, alexandrines, sapphics, spenserian (stanza), etc.

Names of genus and species

In botanical and zoological works the name of a genus should be capitalized and the species printed with the lower-case initial: *Ranunculus fluitans.*

SMALL CAPITALS

FOR some abbreviations small capitals are usual. In printing these no space should be put between the letters:

A.U.C. Anno urbis conditae

A.D. Anno Domini   A.M. Anno mundi

A.H. Anno Hegirae   B.C. Before Christ

a.m. (ante meridiem), p.m. (post meridiem), should be in lower case, exdept in lines of capitals or small capitals.

Text references to capital symbols in plates and line-blocks to be in small capitals, except in scientific work, where capitals are used.

DIVISION OF WORDS

AVOID divisions if at all possible, having regard for the requirements of typography (even spacing, etc.). Not to inconvenience the reader must always be one of the main considerations. The following rules and recommendations apply whenever possible: to avoid uneven spacing, however, one-syllable divisions of two letters are permissible (this should not be necessary in other than the narrowest measures).

Divide according to etymology, where this is obvious: atmo-sphere, bio-graphy, tele-phone, transport, un-equal. Where etymological composition is not obvious divide according to pronunciation; and, in general, break between two (or more) consonants coming together; where there is only one consonant it should normally be taken over:

abs-cess	Euro-pean	minis-ter
abs-tract	forget-ting	ob-scure
ana-lyse	haemor-rhage	philo-sophy
chil-dren	illus-trate	popu-lar
depen-dent	imme-diate	pri-mary
des-tiny	impor-tance	prob-lem
em-brace	inexpli-cable	sem-blance
estab-lish	inter-pret	thou-sand

but do not divide two consonants which form one sound: calm-est, debt-ors, de-scend, fea-ther (but post-humous), lamb-like (but lam-bent), laugh-able, poign-ant, tough-ish, wash-able, and ch whether sounded as in ach-ing or as in poa-cher.

The following divisions are obligatory:

appear-ance	dimin-ish	origin-ally
cele-brate	dis-connect	prob-ably
corre-spon-dence	episco-pal	prop-erly
de-scribe	gener-ally	pun-ish
de-spise	inter-est	

The endings -ism, -ist, -istic may be taken over,

as: human-ism, botan-ist, character-istic; but note neo-logism, criti-cism (and so all words ending in -cism).

In present participles take over -ing, as: carry-ing, crown-ing, divid-ing, toll-ing; but chuck-ling, puz-zling, trick-ling, and similar words.

The terminations -cial, -cian, -cious, -gious, -sion, -tial, -tion should not be divided when forming one sound, as in condescen-sion, espe-cially, forma-tion, Gre-cian, pugna-cious.

Words ending in -logy, -logist: archaeo-logy, etymo-logy, philo-logist, psycho-logist, tauto-logy are normally thus divided; but zoolo-gist.

Avoid divisions which might confuse or alter the meaning, the only permissible divisions of the following being: le-gends (not *leg-ends*), re-adjust (*read-just*), re-appear (*reap-pear*), an exact-ing (*ex-acting*) director, the old umbrella was re-covered and the lost one recovered (indivisible in this context).

Break hyphenated words at the hyphen (avoid introducing a second hyphen): counter-clockwise *not* counter-clock-wise. One-word compounds should be divided at the point of union: railway-man *not* rail-wayman. Divide between vowels only when they are sounded separately: cre-ate, crea-ture.

Many compound scientific words, especially concerning anatomy, biology, and chemistry, are difficult when composition is not known. Divide at the hyphen if hyphenated—otherwise at the point of union. Generally one can divide after such forms as angio-, broncho-, cervico-, deutero-, dia-, glycero-, ophthalmo-, proto-, pseudo-; but note pseud-onym.

A divided word should not end a right-hand page, if it is possible to avoid it.

For a fuller treatment of this problem, see K. Sisam's *Word Division* (S.P.E. Tract No. XXXIII, 1929). The divisions noted as preferable are not free from objection, and should be avoided when it is at all easy to do so.

There are special rules for the division of words in Bibles.

ERRATA, ERRATUM

NOTE that Errata, Addenda, and Corrigenda are plurals, and should only be used when listing a number of items; if there is only one, or when the list has been reduced to one by printing cancels, etc., the heading should be Erratum, Addendum, or Corrigendum.

There should be no point at the end of a line if the point forms no part of the correction; e.g. *for* at *read* near

But the point is sometimes the essential part of the correction, and then must be inserted; e.g. *for* Jones, *read* Jones.

FIGURES AND NUMERALS

WORDS OR FIGURES

DO not mix old-style and new-face figures in the same book without special directions.

Nineteenth century, not 19th century.

Figures to be used when the matter consists of a sequence of stated quantities, particulars of age, etc.

Examples (for non-technical work):

Figures for September show the supply to have been 85,690 tons, a decrease in the month of 57 tons. The past 12 months show a net increase of 5 tons.

The smallest tenor suitable for ten bells is D flat, of 5 feet diameter and 42 cwt.

This applies generally to all units of measurement—tons, cwt., feet, as above, also of area, volume, time, force, electrical units, etc.

Separate objects, animals, ships, persons, etc., are not units of measurement unless they are treated statistically:

A four-cylinder engine of 48 b.h.p. compared with a six-cylinder engine of 65 b.h.p.

The peasant had only four cows.

A farm with 40 head of cattle.

Jellicoe's fleet consisted of twenty-four battleships against the German twenty-two, but six of the latter were pre-dreadnoughts. [Each battleship is identifiable individually; they are not simply units of measurement.]

But:

British losses were: sunk: 3 battle-cruisers, 3 cruisers, and 8 destroyers; and in casualties, killed and missing, 6,097; wounded, 510. [Here the losses of ships (although identifiable) seem to be rather units of measurement. The men killed and wounded, though individuals, are from the military point of view clearly casualties —units of measurement.]

In descriptive matter, numbers under 100 to be in words; but print '90 to 100', not 'ninety to 100'.

Spell out in such instances as:

With God a thousand years are but as one day.

I have said so a hundred times.

For fractions which are spelt out, print, e.g., three-quarters, two-thirds. When both a whole number and a fraction are spelt out, use a hyphen only in the fraction, e.g. one and three-quarters. Print combinations like half an inch, half a dozen, two and six, without hyphens.

NUMERALS GENERALLY

Insert commas with four or more figures, as 7,642 (but see p. 55); print dates without commas, as 1908; omit commas in figures denoting pagination and column numbers, numbering of verse, and in mathematical workings, even though there may be more than three figures; also in library numbers, as: Harleian MS. 24456.

Note a^8 (sheet) and a8 (leaf) in bibliographical matter.

Roman numerals to be preferred in such cases as Henry VIII—which should never be divided; and should not be followed by a full point unless the number ends a sentence. If, however, the author prefers the full title, use 'Henry the Eighth', not 'Henry the VIIIth'.

Use a raised point (·) to express decimals, as 7·06; and print 0·76, *not* ·76. When the time of day is intended to be shown, the full point (.) is to be used, as 4.30 a.m.

In degrees of temperature print 10·15 °C. (not 10·15° C. or 10°·15 C.).

In dates, print: 25 June 1967.[1] Omit comma between month and year: 'The delay after November 1967 was due to an oversight.'

In references to pagination, dates, etc., use the least number of figures possible; for example, print 42–3, 132–6, 1841–5, 1960–1, 1966/7: but print, e.g., 10–11, *not* 10–1; 16–18, *not* 16–8; 116–18, *not* 116–8, 210–11, *not* 210–1, 314–15, *not* 314–5 (i.e. for the group 10–19 in each hundred). And do not contract dates involving different centuries, e.g. 1798–1810 *not* 1798–810. In displayed matter all dates should be in full: 1960–1961.

In collective numbers: *either* from 280 to 300, *or* 280–300; *not* from 280–300.

---

[1] This will not apply to quotations, nor to reprints of documents. As to the form May 19, 1862, Sir James Murray said, 'This is not logical: 19 May 1862 is. *Begin* at day, *ascend* to month, *ascend* to year; not *begin* at month, *descend* to day, then *ascend* to year.'

Print: 250 B.C.; but when it is necessary to insert A.D. the letters should precede the year, as A.D. 250.[1] Print a B.C. period with full figures, e.g. 185–122 B.C.; but a year of office thus: 117/16 B.C., 49/8 B.C.

When preliminary pages are referred to by lower-case roman numerals, no full points should be used after the numerals. Print: p. ii, pp. iii–x; *not* p. ii., pp. iii.–x.

When references are made to two successive text-pages print pp. 6, 7, if the subject is disconnected in the two pages; but if the subject is continuous from one page to the other then print pp. 6–7. The compositor in this must be guided by his copy. Print pp. 51 f. if the reference is to p. 51 and following page; but pp. 51 ff. when the reference is to more than a single page following.

In a sequence of figures use an en rule (–), as in the above examples; so also in such cases as Chapters III–VIII.

Begin numbered paragraphs: 1. 2. etc.; and clauses in paragraphs: (1) (2) (3), etc. If Greek or roman or italic lower-case letters are written, the compositor must follow copy. Roman numerals (I, II, III) are usually reserved for chapters or important sections.

References in the text to footnotes should be made by superior figures, which are to be placed outside the punctuation or quotation mark. Asterisks, superior letters, etc., may be used in special cases. The dagger and the other signs († ‡ § ¶ ||) should be used in mathematical works, to avoid confusion with the workings.

INDEXES

EACH index is considered in relation to the book of which it is a part, and to the use required of it—

---

[1] But print: first century A.D.

which may vary from the simple Name and Place Index to the multiple special indexes of research publications and learned journals. Works on history and literature usually present a third category (of General Index) acting as a clearing-house of the information spread through perhaps many volumes of a wide-ranging work. The following recommendations are neither rigid instructions nor anything more than a starting-point for designing an individual index.

The index should begin on a right-hand page (but may begin on a left-hand page if necessary to make a fit or to avoid an oddment), and any subsequent indexes run on—if necessary on the same page (this again may depend on the fit of index to signatures). There is a tendency for specialized indexes to precede the general index.

The *heading* INDEX should be set in the same style as the book's preliminary titles.

The *page number* is not to appear on the opening page (if not set on chapter opening pages).

The left and right *headlines* throughout should be INDEX (or GENERAL INDEX, SUBJECT INDEX, INDEX OF PLACES, etc.).

The *number of columns* is usually two, but this can be varied to suit length of entries and width of page: only an index of first lines is normally set to the full measure. If there is adequate space between columns, there is no need to insert a rule.

Leaders (. . .) from items to page numbers are not used: page numbers are set close to their items.

Type: usually roman, at least one size smaller than text size, often the same as footnotes. Entries should be set solid by alphabetical sections (q.v.), with close word-spacing. Main references may be indicated by bold type and text-illustration numbers by italic, with roman capitals for plate numbers; but special type for keywords is not used normally. Phrases such as *see*, *see also*, etc., in italic.

Alphabetical sections: insert generally a line of white between sections. A displayed capital may be inserted if specifically asked for.

Entries (keywords, headwords) begin full left with lower case, unless proper names. The keyword should be followed by a comma, and the whole entry usually has a comma before the figures of the page reference. Indent turnover lines 1 em. (See *Sub-entries*.)

Page reference figures should be separated by commas, *groups* of references by semicolons. A colon may be used to separate a keyword from explanatory matter, before the page references. Items in the run-on index (see *Repeated keywords*) are separated by semicolons. It is preferable to omit the full point at the end of a complete entry (except when this forms part of an abbreviation).

See Collins, *Authors' and Printers' Dictionary*, 10th ed. (1956), 'Index', pp. 196 f., for more systems of punctuation. Generally, however, *the less punctuation, the better*.

Sub-entries. There are two methods employed: (*a*) each sub-entry is run-on after the keyword, keeping an indention of 1 em throughout after the first line. Items are separated by semicolons. Thus sub-headings are not used. Advantages: simpler, space-saving. Disadvantage: time-consuming in use. (*b*), which is the more elaborate system, may use more space, but is quicker to consult. The keyword or key-phrase terminates in either comma or colon (see *Entries*, *Page reference figures*), and is set full left. Each sub-entry should begin on a separate line, 1 em indented, with turnovers 2 ems. Further sub-sub-entries may begin on separate lines, 2 ems indented, with turnovers 3 ems (note that turnovers should be 3 ems throughout entries where sub-sub-entries occur). These deep indentions may be avoided by running on sub-sub-entries, separating items by semicolons, turnovers remaining at 2 ems.

Whichever is adopted, (*a*) or (*b*), sub-entries should be either in alphabetical order or in numerical order of the first page reference figure under each.

Repeated keywords. The spaces of indention imply repetition of keywords and sub-headings. This may also be indicated by em rules: these are set full out and repeated as required, with a thin space between. Each rule replaces the keyword or the sub-heading, as marked out by punctuation (see *Entries*).

Turnover. As a general rule the keyword(s), with the addition of '(*cont.*):', should be repeated *only* at the top of the first column of a turnover (left-hand) page, set full left in a separate line. This rule will apply both to indexes with indented sub-entries and to indexes using em rules to indicate repetition of keywords (but see next paragraph). A '(*cont.*)' line will also be inserted where a left-hand page begins with a broken entry, even when it contains only a few lines. (In a *complicated* sequence of sub- and sub-sub-entries it may be helpful to repeat at the top of each column, but in this case special directions will be given.)

Where em-rules are used to indicate the repetition of keywords, they should be retained at the heads of columns, with a '(*cont.*)' line inserted at the top of a left-hand column of a left-hand page (see above). The keyword, however, not a rule, will be placed at the top of the left-hand column of a left-hand page if the entry introduces a completely different person, or place, or subject with the same name, when it would be illogical to insert a '(*cont.*)' line.

Mixture of two or more methods of dealing with sub-entries must be avoided.

ITALIC AND ROMAN TYPE

Use italic for:

Book titles: *Pride and Prejudice, The Origin of Species,* or, Darwin's *Origin of Species, Robinson Crusoe* (the novel; but Robinson Crusoe the character in it).

Film and play titles: *Hamlet, Romeo and Juliet.*

Works of art: Picasso's *Guernica,* the *Discobolus.*

Long poems which are virtually books in themselves: *The Faerie Queene, Paradise Lost, The Lady of the Lake,* Dante's *Paradiso,* and any other poems divided into books or cantos.

Names of periodicals: apparent inconsistency is often caused by the prefix *The* being sometimes printed in italic and sometimes in roman. As a rule, print the definite article in roman lower case, as the *Telegraph,* the *Daily Express. The Times* and *The Economist* are to be exceptions, as those publications prefer to have it so. *The,* if it is part of the title of a book, should also be in italic.[1] The title of an article appearing in a periodical should be in roman within quotation marks (but quotation marks may be omitted in bibliographies or lists of references).

Names of ships: in this case, print 'the' in roman, as it is often uncertain whether 'the' is part of the

[1] Henry Bradley and W. A. Craigie, joint editors of the *O.E.D.,* laid down the following rule: 'When the writer's intention is to quote the exact title as it stands, the article should be printed *The*; but when a work or periodical is merely referred to either as well known to the reader or as having been already mentioned, then the article should be left in roman (without initial capital, if not at the beginning of a sentence).'

title or not. For example, the *King George V*, the *Revenge*; also put other prefixes in roman, as H.M.S. *Dreadnought*. The possessive 's' to be also in roman, e.g. the *Majestic*'s crew. (See also p. 10.)

Stage directions in plays.

Words and short phrases in foreign languages (unless anglicized): in particular this makes clear that a word is foreign when there is an English word spelt the same, e.g. the *Land* governments in West Germany (that is, those of the *Länder* which form the Federal Republic).

In mathematical works theorems are usually printed in italic.

In medical works such terms as *B. influenzae*, *B. subtilis*, *S. haemolyticus* are usually printed in italic.

For italic in musical works see p. 27.

Certain Latin words and their abbreviated forms: *ante*, *c.* (*circa*), *infra*, *passim*, *post*, *sic*, *supra*, *vide*. (Authors and editors should be encouraged to use rather the English forms for most of these: above, below, see, not *supra*, *infra*, *vide*. Sometimes, however, there is no exact equivalent, as for *passim* and *sic*). Italic *s.* and *d.* for shillings (*solidi*) and pence (*denarii*) come in this category (for decimal currency see p. 80).

Use roman in quotation marks for:

Titles of chapters in books, articles in periodicals, shorter poems (not long enough to be treated as book titles, see above), and short extracts from a text (italic being reserved for the title of the over-all work): the 'Ode on the Intimations of Immortality' in *Lyrical Ballads*; D. E. Nineham's articles on 'Oral Tradition' in the *Journal of Theological Studies*; the famous chapter in *The Natural History of Ireland* entitled 'Concerning Snakes' which reads: 'There are no snakes to be met with throughout the whole island.'

Use roman (without quotation marks) for:

House names and public houses: The Firs, the Red Lion (see p. 43).

All the commonest short abbreviations: ad loc., app. crit., cf. (confer, compare), ed. cit., e.g., et seq., ib., ibid., id., i.e., l.c., loc. cit., op. cit., q.v., sc., s.v., viz.,[1] unless otherwise directed.

FOREIGN WORDS AND PHRASES
IN ITALIC AND ROMAN

THE following to be printed in italic:

ab extra	*casus belli*	*en masse*
ab origine	*ceteris paribus*	*en passant*
ad hoc	*chef-d'œuvre*	*en rapport*
ad nauseam	*chevaux de frise*	*en route*
ad valorem	*con amore*	*entente cordiale*
affaire (de cœur)	*consommé*	*esprit de corps*
aficionado	*coup de grâce*	*ex cathedra*
a fortiori	*coup de main*	*ex officiis*
agape (love)	*coup d'état*	*ex officio* (adv.
amende honorable	*coup d'œil*	and adj.)
amour propre	*crime passionnel*	*ex parte*[2] (adv.
ancien régime	*curriculum vitae*	and adj.)
anglice	*démarche*	*facile princeps*
Angst	*demi-monde*	*factum est*
a priori	*demi-tasse*	*fait accompli*
au courant	*de quoi vivre*	*felo de se*
au fond	*de rigueur*	*garçon*
au revoir	*déshabillé*	*grand monde*
bête noire	*dolce far niente*	*habitué*
billet doux	*double entendre*	*hors de combat*
bonhomie	*double entente*	*imprimatur*
bon mot (pl. *bons*	*édition de luxe*	*imprimis*
mots)	*élan*	*in camera*
bon ton	*émigré*	*in propria persona*
brouhaha	*en bloc*	*in situ*
carte blanche	*en fête*	*in vitro*

[1] This expression, although a symbol rather than an abbreviation, must be printed with a full point after the *z*.

[2] Not italic for legal phrase: an ex-parte statement.

in vivo
jeu d'esprit
laissez-faire
laissez-passer
lapsus linguae
lèse-majesté
mise en scène
modus operandi
modus vivendi
mores
more suo
multum in parvo
naïveté
née
nemine
  contradicente
ne plus ultra

noblesse oblige
nolens volens
nom de plume
non est
par excellence
pari passu
per capita
per contra
per se
pièce de résistance
pied-à-terre
post mortem (adv.)
pro forma
pro rata
pro tempore
raison d'être
rapprochement

réchauffé
sans cérémonie
sans-culotte
señor
sensu stricto
sine anno
sine die
sine qua non
sotto voce
status quo
sub rosa
tabula rasa
tour de force
tout court
trompe-l'œil
ultra vires
vis-à-vis

The modern practice is to omit stresses from Latin words.

For further directions as to the use of italic for foreign words and phrases see p. 23.

Print the following anglicized words in roman:

aide-de-camp
al fresco
alias
apache
apartheid
apropos
attaché
aurora borealis
beau idéal
bezique
bizarre
blasé
blitzkrieg
bloc
bona fide

bourgeois
bourgeoisie
bric-à-brac
café
canard
cap-à-pie
carte-de-visite
chargé d'affaires
chateau
chatelaine
chiaroscuro
claque
cliché
clientele
communiqué

concierge
confrère
contretemps
cortège[1]
crèche
crêpe
cul-de-sac
Daiquiri
débâcle
debris
début
débutant(e)
denouement
depot
detour

[1] For a statement as to this and other French words now printed with a grave accent see pp. 90–1.

dilettante
doyen
dramatis
  personae
éclair
éclat
élite
ennui
ensemble
entourage
entrée
entrepôt
entrepreneur
ersatz
espresso
extempore
façade
fête
fiancé(e)
flair
fleur-de-lis
foyer
fracas
furore
gendarme
genre
gratis
habeas corpus
hors-d'œuvre
incommunicado

intransigent
lacuna
levee
literati
littérateur
matinée
mêlée
ménage
menu
milieu
motif
naïve
nuance
obit
  (*noun*)
pakeha
papier mâché
parvenu
passe-partout
patois
per annum
plebiscite
poste restante
post-mortem
  (*adj. and*
  noun)
potpourri
précis
prie-dieu
prima facie

procès-verbal
protégé
provenance
raconteur
recherché
reconnaissance
regime
résumé
reveille
role
sang-froid
savant
seance
seriatim
soirée
sputnik
subpoena
suede
terra firma
tête-à-tête
vade-mecum
verbatim
versus
via
vice versa
virtuoso
visa, visé
viva voce
volte-face
wagon-lit

MUSICAL WORKS

INITIAL capitals should be used for Piano, String, etc., when part of a title of a work, e.g. Brahms's Piano Quintet, op. 25, Beethoven's String Quartet, op. 59, No. 3; but Dvořák's Quintet for piano and strings. Also for First, Second, etc., if, again, it forms part of the generally accepted title of a work, e.g. Brahms's First Piano Concerto; but Cherubini's fifth quartet, since the two words do not form a title in everyday usage.

Where one word, as Allegro, Adagio, is used as a colloquial substitute for 1st movement, etc., print in roman unquoted, and with initial capital. If more than one word, e.g. 'allegro non troppo', 'andante cantabile', use quotation marks and lower-case initials. Use roman and quotes for such phrases as: the long passage 'piu tranquillo', the section 'senza misura'.

Such terms as Finale, Trio, Coda, etc., when used specifically, i.e. as a title used by the composer, to have an initial capital; otherwise, lower-case initial.

Terms such as andante, forte, piano, allegretto, rallentando, etc., to be roman; but *pp*, *ff*, etc.

In general work first and chief words should be capitalized in titles of musical works.

Song titles to be roman and quoted.

Subject-titles to be italic: Gounod's *Faust* (but Bach's Fantasia and Fugue in G minor); Wagner's *Die Meistersinger*; Berlioz's *Symphonie Fantastique*; Parry's *Judith*, etc. But 'New World' Symphony, 'Eroica' Symphony, 'Paris' Symphony, etc. Such titles as the following to be roman: Beethoven's Choral Symphony, Ninth Symphony, etc.

opus 4, no. 2, or op. 4, no. 2, to be printed thus.

Technical names of periods or styles to have lower-case initial: organum, descant, polyphony, etc.

Names of instruments and organ stops to be roman: cor anglais, cornet-à-piston, timpani; diapason, vox humana.

Leitmotif, motif, to be anglicized thus, and roman.

Print quartet, quintet, not quartette, etc.

Model sentence: The Allegro of Dvořák's First Piano Concerto, unlike the 'adagio giocoso e non legato' of Tchaikovsky's Sonata for viola d'amore and spinet, begins with a coda, reminiscent of his earlier song 'Aufenthalt', which itself is based on the 'senza misura' passage in the Scherzo of his last symphonic poem, *The Lion-Tamers*.

NOR AND OR

PRINT: (1) Neither one nor the other; neither Jew nor Greek; neither Peter nor James. (2) Either one or the other; either Jew or Greek; either Peter or James.

Never print: Neither one or the other; neither Peter or James; but when the sentence is continued to a further comparison, 'nor' and 'or' must be printed (in the continuation) according to the sense.

Likewise note that for singular subjects the verb should be in the singular, as 'Neither Oxford nor Reading *is* stated to have been represented.'

O AND OH

WHEN used in addressing persons or things in the vocative, 'O' is printed with a capital and without any point following it; e.g. 'O mighty Caesar! dost thou lie so low'; 'O world! thou wast the forest to this hart'; 'O most bloody sight!' Similarly, 'O Lord', 'O God'. But when not used in the vocative it should be spelt 'Oh', and is usually separated from what follows by a punctuation mark; e.g. 'Oh, pardon me, thou bleeding piece of earth'; 'For if you should, oh! what would come of it?' Where, however, there is no pause in an exclamatory phrase, the comma is omitted; e.g. 'Oh that my words were now written! Oh that they were inscribed in a book!'

POETRY

WORDS ending in -ed are to be so spelt; a grave accent is sometimes used when the syllable is separately pronounced, thus: -èd.

This applies to poetical quotations in prose matter, and to new works. It must not apply to reprints of standard authors, nor to quotations in works which reproduce old spellings, etc. Neither must it apply to poems in which an author prefers his own method.

Whenever a poetic quotation is given a line (or more) to itself, it is not to be placed within quotation marks; but when the line of poetry runs on with the prose, or when a number of quotations follow one another and it is necessary to distinguish them, then quotation marks are to be used.

POSSESSIVE CASE

USE 's for the possessive case in English names and surnames whenever possible; i.e. in all monosyllables and disyllables, and in longer words accented on the penult as:

Charles's	Jones's
Cousins's	Thomas's
Gustavus's	St. Thomas's
Hicks's	Thoms's
St. James's Square	Zacharias's

In longer names not accented on the penult, 's is also preferable, though ' is here admissible; e.g. Theophilus'.

But poets in all these cases sometimes use s' only; and Jesus' is an accepted liturgical archaism. In quotations from Scripture follow the Oxford standard.

In ancient classical names use s' (not s's): Mars', Venus', Herodotus'. This is the prevailing custom in classical works.

Likewise ancient names in -es are usually written -es' in the possessive:

Ceres' rites	Xerxes' fleet

This form should certainly be used in words longer than two syllables:

Arbaces'	Miltiades'
Cervantes'	Themistocles'

To pronounce another 's (= ez) after these is difficult.

This applies only to *ancient* words. One writes Moses' law; and I used to alight at Moses's for the British Museum.

As to the latter example, Moses, the tailor, was a modern man, like Thomas and Lewis; and in using his name we follow modern English usage.

French names ending in s or x should always be followed by 's when used possessively in English. Thus, it being taken for granted that the French pronunciation is known to the ordinary reader, and using Rabelais = Rabelè, Hanotaux = Hanotō, Le Roux = Le Roo, Dumas = Dumah, as examples, the only correct way of writing these names in the possessive in English is Rabelais's (= Rabelèz), Hanotaux's (= Hanotōz), Le Roux's (= Le Rooz), Dumas's (= Dumahz).

An apostrophe must not be used with the pronouns hers, ours, theirs, yours, its.

Apostrophes in place-names.[1] 1. Use an apostrophe after the 's' in Queens' College (Camb.). But:

2. Use an apostrophe before the 's' in: Connah's Quay (Flints.), Hunter's Quay (Arg.), Land's End, Lord's Ground, Orme's Head (Caerns.), The Queen's College (Oxford), St. Abb's Head (Bwk.), St. John's (Newfoundland), St. John's Wood (London), St. Michael's Mount (Cornwall), St. Mungo's Well (Knaresboro'), St. Peter's (Sydney, N.S.W.).

[1] The selection is arbitrary: but the examples are given on the authority of the Oxford University and Cambridge University Calendars, the *Post Office Guide*, *Crockford's Clerical Directory*, and the gazetteers in the Oxford Atlases.

3. Do not use an apostrophe in: All Souls (Oxford), Bury St. Edmunds, Earls Court, Golders Green, Husbands Bosworth (Rugby), Johns Hopkins University (U.S.A.), Millers Dale (Derby), Owens College (Manchester), St. Andrews, St. Albans, St. Bees, St. Boswells, St. Helens (Lancs.), St. Ives (Hunts. and Cornwall), St. Kitts (St. Christopher Island, W.I.), St. Leonards, St. Neots (Hunts. but St. Neot, Cornwall), Somers Town (London).

PROOF CORRECTION

This section and some others (e.g. Scientific Work, pp. 52 ff.) are intended to be of assistance to authors, editors, and others who prepare manuscripts and handle proofs for the Press.

Corrections

Use ink or ball-point (avoid the use of pencil). Corrections should be written in the margins, marks in the text merely indicating where the corrections are to be made.

The cost of corrections will be reduced if alterations can be so phrased as to fit approximately to the space left by deleted words.

Lengthy insertions are best typed on a separate sheet and attached to the proof, their positions being clearly indicated in the text.

Draw a stroke (/) after each marginal mark to show that the correction is concluded. This is important where there are several corrections in a line.

Directions

Matter other than corrections (i.e. instructions to the printer or comments) should be preceded by the word 'PRINTER', and encircled. A different coloured ink is helpful for this purpose.

PROOF-CORRECTION MARKS

Instruction to Printer	Textual mark	Marginal mark
Insert new matter	ʌ	New matter followed by concluding stroke (/)
Delete	Stroke through character(s) to be deleted	♂
Correction made in error. Leave as printed	..... under character(s) to remain	*stet*
Change to capital(s)	≡ under character(s) to be changed	*cap(s)*
Change to small capital(s)	= under character(s) to be changed	*s.c.*
Change to lower case (small letters)	Encircle character(s) to be changed	*l.c.*
Change to bold type	∼∼ under character(s) to be changed	*bold*
Change to roman type	Encircle character(s) to be changed	*rom.*
Change to italic type	― under character(s) to be changed	*ital.*
Insert rule under this (these) character(s)	― under character(s) affected	(*Printer : insert rule*)
(Wrong fount) Replace by character(s) of correct fount	Encircle character(s) to be changed	*w.f.*
Invert block or character(s)	Encircle block or character(s) to be altered	♀
Replace damaged character(s)	― under character(s) to be changed	×

(A multiplication sign should be indicated thus: × (*multiple*))

Substitute or insert 'superior' character(s)	Stroke through character(s) to be changed, or ⋀ where required	⋎ under character (e.g. ²⁄₉)
Substitute or insert 'inferior' character(s)	Stroke through character(s) to be changed, or ⋀ where required	⋏ over character (e.g. $z^?$)
Use ligature fl, etc. or diphthong æ, etc.	Stroke through characters to be changed	*fl* (one piece) *æ* (one piece)
Insert space	⋀, or ⟩ if between lines	#
(N.B. Several combinations are possible: less #, more #, eq. (equal) #, etc.)		
Insert spaces between letters	⏑⏑⏑⏑ between tops of letters to be spaced	*letter* #
Rearrange characters or words in correct order	⌐ between characters or words to be transposed, numbered where necessary	*trs.*/
Rearrange to make a new paragraph here	⌊ before first word of new paragraph	*n. p.*
Rearrange: no fresh paragraph here	⌒ between paragraphs	*run on*
Insert hyphen	⋏	|-|
Insert en-rule	⋏	en
Insert em-rule	⋏	em
Insert apostrophe	⋏	⸜
Substitute or insert comma, semicolon, etc.	Stroke through character to be changed, or ⋀ where required	, ; / ⊙ / ⊙ / ? / ! / ; / ⟨ / ⟩ / ⌈ / ⌉ ...

MARKS USED IN THE
CORRECTION OF PROOFS

Adapted from JOHNSON's *Typographia* (1824),
Vol. II, p. 216

THOUGH a variety of opinions exist as to *a/*
the individual by whom the art of printing was *9*
first discovered; yet all authorities concur
caps./   in admitting Peter Schoeffer to be the person
who invented *cast metal types*, having learned
the art of p̶u̶ *cutting* the letters from the Guty- *8/*
tembergs/ he is also supposed to have been
the first who engraved on copper/plates. The *|-|*
following testimony is preserved in the family, *r/*
LLLLL   by |Jo. |Fred. |Faustus |of |Ascheffenburg:
n.p.   [Peter Schoeffer of Gernsheim, perceiving *s.c./*
his master Fausts design, and being himself
trs./ |desirous⁀ardently| to improve the art, found
out (by the good providence of God) the
method of cutting (*incidendi*) the characters
in a *matrix*, that the letters might easily be
singly *cast,* instead of b̶e̶i̶n̶g *cut.* He pri- *trs./*
vately *cut matrices* for the whole alphabet:
Faust was so pleased with the contrivance
that he promised Peter to give him his only *w.f.*
daughter Christina in marriage, a promise *ital/*
which he soon after performed.   (*run on*)
as/   But there were/ many difficulties at first
rom./   with these (*letters*), as there had been before
ital./   with wooden ones/ the metal being too soft
to support the force of the im⁀pression: but
this defect was soon remedied, by mixing
trs./ |a substance⁀with |the metal| which sufficiently *;/*
hardened it/'

*and when he showed his master
the letters cast from these matrices,*

THE OPPOSITE PAGE
CORRECTED

From JOHNSON'S *Typographia* (1824),
Vol. II, p. 217

THOUGH a variety of opinions exist as to
the individual by whom the art of printing was
first discovered; yet all authorities concur
in admitting PETER SCHOEFFER to be
the person who invented *cast metal types*,
having learned the art of *cutting* the letters
from the Guttembergs: he is also supposed to
have been the first who engraved on copper-
plates. The following testimony is preserved
in the family, by Jo. Fred. Faustus of Aschef-
fenburg:

'PETER SCHOEFFER of Gernsheim, perceiving his master Faust's design, and being
himself ardently desirous to improve the art,
found out (by the good providence of God) the
method of cutting (*incidendi*) the characters
in a *matrix*, that the letters might easily be
singly *cast*, instead of being *cut*. He pri-
vately *cut matrices* for the whole alphabet:
and when he showed his master the letters
cast from these matrices, Faust was so pleased
with the contrivance that he promised Peter
to give him his only daughter *Christina* in
marriage, a promise which he soon after performed. But there were as many difficulties
at first with these letters, as there had been
before with *wooden ones*; the metal being too
soft to support the force of the impression:
but this defect was soon remedied, by mixing
the metal with a substance which sufficiently
hardened it.'

Queries

To accept a reader's query, strike out the question mark, leaving the correction that is to be made, thus:

To remove any possible doubt 'Yes' may be written against it.

To reject a reader's query, strike out the whole query and write 'No' against it, thus:

PUNCTUATION

Comma

Generally, commas should be inserted between adjectives preceding and qualifying a substantive, as:

An enterprising, ambitious man.

A gentle, amiable, harmless creature.

A cold, damp, badly lighted room.

But where the last adjective is in closer relation to the substantive than the preceding ones, omit the comma, as:

A distinguished foreign author.

The sailor was accompanied by a great rough Newfoundland dog.

Where *and* joins two single words or phrases the comma is usually omitted:

The honourable and learned member.

But where more than two words or phrases occur together in a sequence a comma should precede the *and*:

A great, wise, and beneficent measure.

The following sentence, containing two conjunctive *and*'s, needs no commas:

God is wise and righteous and faithful.

In such sentences as the following use a comma:

Truth ennobles man, and learning adorns him.

The Parliament is not dissolved, but only prorogued.

I believed, and therefore I spoke.

The question is, Can it be performed?

My son, give me thy heart.

The Armada being thus happily defeated, the nation resounded with shouts of joy.

Virtue is the highest proof of a superior understanding, and the only basis of greatness.

In some cases, however, two or more commas are necessary:

The French, having occupied Portugal, began to advance into Spain.

Be assured, then, that order, frugality, and economy are the necessary supporters of every personal and private virtue.

Such words as moreover, however, etc., are usually followed by a comma when used as the first word of a sentence, and preceded and followed by a comma when used later in a sentence. For instance:

In any case, however, the siphon may be filled.

Commas are often used instead of parentheses:

Perhaps the most masterly, and certainly the easiest, presentation of the thought is in the Prelude.

When a preposition assumes the character of an adverb a comma should follow it, to avoid awkwardness or ambiguity:

In the valley below, the villages looked very small.

Omit the comma in such phrases as 'my friend Lord Oxford', 'my friend the Chancellor of the Exchequer'.

Omit the comma when printing house numbers in addresses: 44 High Street.

Semicolon

The semicolon separates two or more clauses which are of more or less equal importance and are linked as a pair or series:

> Truth ennobles man; learning adorns him.

> Economy is no disgrace; for it is better to live on a little than to outlive a great deal.

> The temperate man's pleasures are always durable, because they are regular; and all his life is calm and serene, because it is innocent.

> Those faults which arise from the will are intolerable; for dull and insipid is every performance where inclination bears no part.

> To err is human; to forgive, divine.

> Never speak concerning what you are ignorant of; speak little of what you know; and whether you speak or say not a word, do it with judgement.

Semicolons divide the simple members of a compound sentence, and a dash may follow the last clause before the general conclusion:

> To give an early preference to honour above gain, when they stand in competition; to despise every advantage which cannot be attained without dishonest arts; to brook no meanness, and stoop to no dissimulation—these are the indications of a great mind.

The sign ⸴ (*punctus elevatus*),[1] which occurs occasionally in Old English manuscripts and frequently
in Middle English manuscripts, is not a semicolon
and should not be replaced by ;.

Colon

Whereas the semicolon links equal or balanced
clauses, the colon generally marks a step forward,
from introduction to main theme, from cause to
effect, premiss to conclusion, etc. It is regularly
used to introduce examples, as here:

> In business there is something more than barter,
>   exchange, price, payment: there is a sacred
>   faith of man in man.
>
> Study to acquire a habit of thinking: no study is
>   more important.
>
> Always remember the ancient maxim: Know
>   thyself.

A dash should not be added to a colon which is
being used to introduce a list.

Full point[2]

Examples of its ordinary use:

> Fear God. Honour the King. Pray without ceasing.
>
> There are thoughts and images flashing across the
>   mind in its highest moods, to which we give
>   the name of inspiration. But whom do we
>   honour with this title of the inspired poet?

---

[1] The use of the *punctus elevatus* is described by P. Clemoes,
*Liturgical Influence on Punctuation in Late Old English and
Early Middle English Manuscripts* (Cambridge, 1952).

[2] An abbreviation point preceding a quotation mark closes
a sentence and an extra point outside the quote is unnecessary,
e.g. . . . in 'titles of works, etc.' The sentence point is, however,
required after a parenthesis, e.g. . . . titles (of works, etc.).

Question mark

Examples of its ordinary use:

> Shall little, haughty ignorance pronounce
> His work unwise, of which the smallest part
> Exceeds the narrow vision of the mind?

> Was the prisoner alone when he was apprehended?
> Is he known to the police? Has he any regular
> occupation?

> What does the pedant mean?

Cases where the note of interrogation must not
be used, the speaker simply stating a fact:

> The Cyprians asked me why I wept.
> I was asked if I would stop for dinner.

Exclamation mark

Examples of its ordinary use:

> Hail, source of Being! universal Soul!
> Alas for his poor family!
> O excellent guardian of the sheep!—a wolf!
> Alas, my noble boy! that thou shouldst die!
> Ah me! she cried, and waved her lily hand.
> O despiteful love! unconstant womankind!

Apostrophe[1]

Apostrophes in contractions similar to the following should join close up to the letters: don't, 'em,
haven't, o'er, shan't, shouldn't, 'tis, won't, there'll,
I'd, I'll, we'll, I've, you've, he's, she's, it's, William's
(William is, has).[2]

---

[1] See also Possessive Case, pp. 29 ff.
[2] See also pp. 107, 108–9.

Parentheses[1]

Examples:

I have seen charity (if charity it may be called)
insult with an air of pity.

Left now to himself (malice could not wish him
a worse adviser), he resolves on a desperate
project.

Occasionally parentheses occur within parentheses, as in the following: (*Wheaton* v. *Peters* (1834),
8 Peters, 591); (Copyright Act, 1911, 6. 26 (2)). In
the latter instance a 1-pt. space should divide the
two parentheses falling together at the end.

Square brackets

These marks are used chiefly to enclose an explana-
tion by someone other than the author. For example:

Perhaps (alarming thought!), perhaps he [Death]
aims
Ev'n now the fatal blow that ends my life.

They [the Lilliputians] rose like one man.

Dash

Em rules or dashes—in this and the next line an
example is given—are often used to show that words
enclosed between them are to be read parenthetically.
In the following example the dashes help to clarify
a somewhat involved sentence:

Early in August M. Krestinski, the Soviet Am-
bassador in Berlin, who in consequence of the
incident had been—not recalled but—granted
leave of absence, returned to his post.

Thus the punctuation of a verbal parenthesis may
be indicated in three ways: by em dashes, by ( ), or
by commas.

[1] Printers call ( ) parentheses, [ ] square brackets, and ⟨ ⟩
angle brackets.

Omit the dash when a colon is used to preface a quotation or similar matter, whether at the end of a break-line or not.

The dash is used to mark an interruption or breaking off in the middle of a sentence.

Marks of omission

To mark omitted words three points . . . (not asterisks) separated by normal space of line are sufficient; and the practice should be uniform throughout the work. Where an initial is omitted as unknown two dots only should be used: such cases occur mainly in printing old documents. Where full lines are required to mark a large omission, real or imaginary, the spacing between the marks should be increased; but the compositor should still use full points, not asterisks.

When three points are used at the end of an incomplete sentence a fourth full point should not be added; normal space of line should precede the first full point. But where the sentence is complete, the closing point is set close up, followed by three points for omission.

Quotation marks

Omit quotation marks for poetry, as instructed on p. 29. Also omit them for prose extracts broken off in smaller type, unless contrary instructions are given. Repeat quotation marks at the beginning of each new paragraph when used.

Insert quotation marks in titles of essays: e.g. 'Mr. Brock read a paper on "Description in Poetry".' But omit quotation marks when the subject of the paper is an author: e.g. 'Professor Bradley read a paper on Jane Austen.' (See also p. 49.)

Quotation marks may be used to enclose slang and technical terms. They should not be used with house names or public houses: Chequers, Cosicot, the Barley Mow.

Single 'quotes' are to be used for the first quotation; then double for a quotation within a quotation. If there should be yet another quotation within the second quotation it is necessary to revert to single quotation marks.

Relative placing of quotation marks and punctuation

All signs of punctuation used with words in quotation marks must be placed *according to the sense*. If an extract ends with a point or exclamation or interrogation sign, let that point be included before the closing quotation mark; but not otherwise. When there is one quotation within another, and both end with the sentence, put the punctuation mark before the first of the closing quotation marks. These are important directions for the compositor to bear in mind; and he should examine the examples given in the pages that follow:

'The passing crowd' is a phrase coined in the spirit of indifference. Yet, to a man of what Plato calls 'universal sympathies', and even to the plain, ordinary denizens of this world, what can be more interesting than those who constitute 'the passing crowd'?

If the physician sees you eat anything that is not good for your body, to keep you from it he cries, 'It is poison!' If the divine sees you do anything that is hurtful for your soul, he cries, 'You are lost!'

'Why does he use the word "poison"?'

But I boldly cried out, 'Woe unto this city!'

Alas, how few of them can say, 'I have striven to the very utmost'!

Thus, notes of exclamation and interrogation are sometimes included in and sometimes follow quotation marks, as in the sentences above, according to whether their application is merely to the words quoted or to the whole sentence of which they form a part. The sentence-stop must be omitted after ? or ! even when the ? or ! precedes the closing quotation marks.

In regard to other points, when a comma, full point, colon, or semicolon is required at the end of a quotation, there is no reason for perpetuating the bad practice of their undiscriminating inclusion within the quotation marks at the end of an extract. So place full points, commas, etc., according to the examples that follow.

(i) Example: Our subject is the age of Latin literature known as 'Silver'. The single word 'Silver', being very far from a complete sentence, cannot have a closing point belonging to it: the point belongs to the whole sentence and should go outside the quotation marks, viz. . . . known as 'Silver'.

(ii) If the quotation is intermediate between a single word and a complete sentence, or it is not clear whether it is a complete sentence or not, judgement must be used in placing the final point:

We need not 'follow a multitude to do evil'.

The words quoted are the greater part of a sentence— '[Do not] follow a multitude to do evil'—but not complete in themselves, so do not require their own closing point; the point therefore belongs to the main sentence, and is outside the quotation marks.

Similarly in:

No one should 'follow a multitude to do evil', as the Scripture says.
Do not 'follow a multitude to do evil'; on the contrary do what is right.

Here the comma and semicolon do not belong to the quoted words and are outside the quotation marks.

(iii) The quoted words may be a complete sentence but the closing point must be omitted because the main sentence is not complete:

You say 'It cannot be done': I say it can.

Here the colon clearly belongs to the main sentence, forming the punctuation between 'You say' and 'I say', and is therefore outside the quotation marks.

(iv) When a quotation is broken off and resumed after such words as 'he said', if it would naturally have had any punctuation at the point where it is broken off, a comma is placed within the quotation marks to represent this.

Example: The words to be quoted are: 'It cannot be done; we must give up the task.' In quotation this might appear as:

'It cannot be done,' he said; 'we must give up the task.'

Note that the comma after 'done' belongs to the quotation, which has a natural pause at this point, but the semicolon has to be placed after 'said' and hence outside the quotation marks.

On the other hand, if the quotation is continuous, without punctuation at the point where it is broken, the comma should be outside the quotation marks.

Example: The words to be quoted are: 'Go home to your father.' In quotation these appear as:

'Go home', he said, 'to your father.'

The comma after 'home' does not belong to the quotation and therefore comes outside the quotation marks.

These rules, though somewhat lengthy to state in full, are simply instances of the maxim—*place punctuation according to sense.*

(v) The quoted words may be a complete sentence which ends at the same point as the main sentence:

> He said curtly, 'It cannot be done.'

Logically, two full points would be required, one inside the quotes belonging to the quoted sentence, and one outside belonging to the main sentence. In such cases the point should be set *inside* the quotation marks (as ! or ? would be) and the point closing the main sentence omitted.

In particular, when a long sentence is quoted, introduced by quite a short phrase, it is better to attach the closing point to the long sentence:

> Jesus said, 'Do not think that I have come to annul the Law and the Prophets; I have come to fulfil them.' (Not '. . . to fulfil them'.)

(vi) Where *more than one sentence* is quoted, the first (and intermediate) sentence(s) will naturally have their closing point(s) within the quotation, and the last sentence should do so also:

> Moses told you: 'Do not kill. Do not steal. Do not commit adultery.' (Not '. . . adultery'.)

(vii) When a quotation is followed by a reference, giving its source, in parentheses, if it is a complete sentence, the closing quote is placed according to the above rules, before the parenthesis, and there is another closing point inside the parentheses:

> 'If the writer of these pages shall chance to meet with any that shall only study to cavil and pick a quarrel with him, he is prepared beforehand to take no notice of it.' (*Works of Charles and Mary Lamb*, Oxford edition, i. 193.)

(viii) Where marks of omission or (more rarely) 'etc.' are used, they should be placed within the quotation marks if it is clear that the omitted matter forms part of the quotation.

Punctuation in classical and philological notes

In notes on English and foreign classics, as a rule[1] follow the punctuation in the following examples:

5. *Falls not*: lets not fall. (That is, a colon is usual after the lemma where a simple definition follows.)

17. *swoon*. The spelling of the folios is 'swound'. (Here a full point is used, because the words that follow the lemma constitute a complete sentence.)

Note that the initial letter of the word or phrase treated (as in *Falls not* and *swoon* above) should be in agreement with the text.

The lemma should be set in italic or bold type, according to directions.

Punctuation marks and references to footnotes in juxtaposition

The relation of these to each other is dealt with on p. 18. Examples of the right practice are to be found on many pages of the present work.

Points in title-pages, headlines, etc.

All points (other than marks of interrogation or exclamation) are to be omitted from the ends of lines in titles, half-titles, page-headings, and cross-headings, unless a special direction is given to the contrary.

QUOTATIONS

QUOTATIONS in prose should not be broken off from the text unless the matter exceeds five lines. But short prose quotations (less than five lines) may be broken off if the context demands it, i.e. if the author sets them out, as it were, as examples or

[1] There are exceptions, as in works which have a settled style of their own.

specimens. Conversely, if the author weaves the quotations into his own paragraphs or even sentences, making it awkward to break them off, even longer extracts can be run on in the text in quotes.

When broken off, i.e. begun on a fresh line with the text on a fresh line following, quotations are distinguished, usually, by setting them in smaller type, full measure. Extracts treated in this way do not need to be enclosed by quotation marks (and therefore any quotations within them should be in single quotation marks, not double for quotes within quotes).

Any words of his own interpolated by the author in a quotation must be set in [ ] to show that they are not part of the quoted matter.

If two or more broken-off quotations follow without the author's own text intervening, and these are not continuous in the original, as there are no quotes to close and reopen the separation must be shown by leading.

If either of the last two paragraphs occasions difficulty, then the quoted matter must be set in (single) quotes in the normal way even though broken off.

The above rules apply to verse quotations with the addition that even a single line of poetry can be broken off, and if so, needs no quotes (but see Poetry, pp. 28 f.).

REFERENCES TO PRINTED AND MANUSCRIPT SOURCES

Printed works

REFERENCES to books should normally be in the form Stubbs, *Constitutional History*, vol. ii, p. 98; or (if the context justifies it, i.e. the reader can be assumed to be familiar with the abbreviated title) Stubbs, *Const. Hist.* ii. 98. (When any abbreviations, other than the most common, such as *O.E.D.*, *D.N.B.*, are used for book titles, they should be listed and explained.) Whichever style is adopted should be uniform throughout the work, except that the system may be used of giving the first reference in full, and abbreviating thereafter.

In science books book-titles, whether appearing in the body of the text, including footnotes, or in bibliographies, 'further reading' lists, etc., will be printed with capital initial letters for the first word and proper names only. In all other classes of work it will be the practice to capitalize the first and all chief words.

The title of an article in a periodical should be printed in roman within single quotation marks, with the important words capitalized, and the title of the periodical (whether abbreviated or not) in italic: E. J. Dobson, 'A New Edition of "The Owl and the Nightingale" ', *Notes and Queries*, ccvi (1961), 444–8. In scientific works, titles of papers are printed without quotation marks, and with capital initials for proper nouns only.

Arabic figures in either bold or ordinary type are used for volume numbers of scientific periodicals. This style is also to be encouraged for references in general works.

An author of a book to be published by the Press is advised to adopt the system of references indicated above.

Mention of the place of publication as well as the publisher is frequently useful to the reader.

Examples (of printed works):

G. Cary, *The Medieval Alexander* (Cambridge, 1956), 54.

M. S. Serjeantson, 'The Dialects of the West Midlands in Middle English', *R.E.S.* iii (1927), 331.

William Twiti, *L'Art de vénerie*, ed. G. Tilander
   (Uppsala, 1956).

Note, as in the above examples, p. for page may
be omitted, especially when there is a volume number, ii. 98 being read as vol. ii, p. 98.

But in some standard works columns are numbered
and ii. 98 would then refer to vol. ii, col. 98. This
should cause no confusion as anyone turning up the
reference will see the printed column numbers but
not page numbers: beware, however, of inserting
'p.' in such cases. The author should be consulted if
necessary.

Citation of authorities at the end of quotations
should be printed thus: HOMER, *Odyssey*, ii. 15, but
print HOR. *Carm.* II. xiv. 2; HOM. *Od.* iv. 272. This
applies chiefly to quotations at the heads of chapters.
It does not refer to frequent citations in notes,
where the author's name is usually in lower case.

In poetry and plays, instead of volume and page,
act and/or scene and line will be referred to, as
follows:

References to Shakespeare's plays thus: *2 Henry
VI*, III. ii. 14; and so with other references to act,
scene, and line.

References to poems divided into books, cantos,
and lines; e.g. Spenser, *Faerie Queene*, IV. xxvi. 35.

References to the Bible in ordinary works to
be printed thus: Job 32: 22; 37: 2, 17; 39: 38–9.
(For full list of abbreviations see pp. 6–7.)

References to MSS. or unprinted documents
should be in roman.

For use of italic see also pp. 22 ff.

In the citation of Acts of Parliament, note the
use of arabic figures for chapter numbers in Public
(General) and Private Acts (e.g. 3 & 4 Geo. V, c. 12,
ss. 18, 19) and small roman numerals in Public
(Local) Acts (e.g. 3 & 4 Geo. V, c. xii, ss. 18, 19).

Scots Acts prior to the Union of 1707 are cited by year (*anno domini*) and chapter, thus: 1532, c. 40.

In references to law reports care should be taken to distinguish between round and square brackets, and also to place the comma correctly. In the Law Reports published by the Incorporated Council of Law Reporting from the year 1891 onwards, the date is a necessary part of the description of the volume, and accordingly, if a comma is used it should come before the date. The date is placed within square brackets, and where there is more than one volume in a year, the number of the volume follows the date: e.g. *Rose* v. *Buckett*, [1901] 2 K.B. 449. The same rule is followed by the Irish Council of Law Reporting from 1894 onwards: e.g. *R.* v. *Allen*, [1921] 2 I.R. 241; and in one or two other series. In almost all other series (including those published by the Incorporated Council of Law Reporting before 1891) the volumes are serially numbered without the date being expressed; but as it is almost impossible to remember off-hand the date of a case cited merely by the volume, in recent books it has become a regular practice, and one to be strongly recommended, to add the date in round brackets after the name of the case, a comma then preceding the description of the volume: e.g. *Croft* v. *Dunphy* (1932), 102 L.J.P.C. 6. Thus the round brackets give real dates, the square often a false date, for cases are not rarely reported in the volume of the year following their delivery. The rule therefore for placing the comma is: round brackets are followed by the comma, square brackets follow it. However, in the Law Reports themselves and in many other publications commas are not used at all.

Cases from the Scottish Series of Session Cases from the year 1907 onwards are cited as follows: e.g. *Hughes* v. *Stewart*, 1907 S.C. 791; Justiciary Cases, from 1917 onwards, as, for example, *Corcoran* v. *H.M. Advocate*, 1932 J.C. 42. It is usual to refer to Justiciary Cases (i.e. criminal cases before the High Court of Justiciary) simply by the name of the panel (or accused), thus: *Corcoran*.

MS. and unpublished sources

References to ancient MSS. subsequently printed (as distinct from the printed editions thereof), old unpublished letters, etc., or modern ones deposited in libraries but not published, should not be set in italic. Examples:

Bodl. MS. Rawlinson D. 520, fo. 7.

MS. Bodley 34, fo. 14^v.

B.M. MS. Cott. Vitellius A. xiv, fo. 10^v.

Lieut. Frewen's Diary, 3 June 1916 (unpublished: but *Diary* would imply that it was published).

Personal letter to the author, 28 Nov. 1964.

B. A. Smith, 'The Influence of the R.C. Church on Anglican Doctrine' (Univ. of Leeds M.A. thesis 1936).

Government and official papers

When printing references to Command Papers, the author's use of Cd., Cmd., and Cmnd. must be followed. These distinctions are significant in that they each represent a different series.

SCIENTIFIC WORK

Copy should be clear. Special mathematical symbols and formulae may on occasion have to be written in by hand. Writing formulae by hand permits more flexibility, but the author should remember that the compositor is a layman, and has no context to guide him; hence the need for care in writing.

Many capital letters (C K M O P S U V W X Y Z)

can easily be confused with lower case; and O, *o*, o, o (fig.); e, l, ɪ; x, X are easily confused unless their size and form are clearly indicated.

Symbols should be unmistakable. Care should be taken to distinguish between italic *a*, Greek *α*; italic *w*, Greek *ω*; and many other confusable characters.

Most mathematical symbols are printed in italic; all chemical symbols in roman. If both occur and there is a danger of confusion, it is helpful if they are so marked.

All mathematical symbols that are not to be printed in italic should be so marked. Since the same letter may be called for in various founts (e.g. bold face for vectors), the standard printer's markings should be used:

single underline x̲ indicates italic *x*

double	,,	x̳	,,	small capital x
treble	,,	x̲̳	,,	capital X
wavy	,,	x̰	,,	bold face **x**
	thus	x̲̳	,,	italic capital *X*

Abbreviations for units, etc., should be consistent. It is recommended that the list in the various parts of the comprehensive British Standard (B.S. 1991 (1967)) be followed.

To reduce hand work (and improve general appearance) two-line fractions in the text should be avoided, e.g. the forms $\frac{a}{b}$, $\left|\frac{x-1}{3}\right|$, etc., should, by the use of the solidus, be replaced by a/b, $|(x-1)/3|$, etc. Simple fractions such as $\frac{\pi}{2}$, $\frac{x}{3}$, $\frac{a+b}{4}$, etc., are best printed as $\frac{1}{2}\pi$, $\frac{1}{3}x$, $\frac{1}{4}(a+b)$, etc.

Displayed formulae three or four lines deep can be reduced to the neater and much more manageable two-line form in almost all instances.

$$\frac{1-\tan^2\dfrac{A}{2}}{1+\tan^2\dfrac{A}{2}} \text{ should be written } \frac{1-\tan^2\tfrac{1}{2}A}{1+\tan^2\tfrac{1}{2}A};$$

$$\frac{\sin\dfrac{(N+1)}{2}\theta\,\sin\dfrac{N}{2}\theta}{\sin\dfrac{\theta}{2}}$$

should be written

$$\frac{\sin\tfrac{1}{2}(N+1)\theta\,\sin\tfrac{1}{2}N\theta}{\sin\tfrac{1}{2}\theta}.$$

Hand work can be reduced and appearance improved by writing such a formula as

$$\lim_{n\to\infty}\left\{1-\sin^2\frac{\alpha}{n}\right\}^{-\overline{\sin^2\frac{\alpha}{n}}}$$

in the form

$$\lim_{n\to\infty}\{1-\sin^2(\alpha/n)\}^{-1/\sin^2(\alpha/n)}.$$

The rule (or vinculum) should be omitted from the square-root sign. Where necessary it may be replaced by parentheses:

e.g. $\sqrt{2}$ is sufficient for $\sqrt{\overline{2}}$

and $\sqrt{\left(\dfrac{x^2}{a^2}+\dfrac{y^2}{b^2}\right)}$ for $\sqrt{\dfrac{x^2}{a^2}+\dfrac{y^2}{b^2}}$,

and in each case the first form is more easily printed.

As far as possible any symbol which involves printing a separate line of type should be avoided when an alternative form is available:

e.g. for angle ABC $\angle ABC$ is preferable to $\widehat{ABC}$

or for vector r **r** (bold type) „   „   „ $\overrightarrow{r}$

Punctuation. A mathematical formula or equation, whether occurring in the text or displayed, should be regarded as in every way an integral part of the sentence in which it occurs, and be punctuated accordingly. Thus, individual formulae may be separated by commas, groups by semicolons, and where a formula occurs at the end of a sentence it should be followed by a full point (full stop).

In the case of displayed chemical formulae, however, especially of the type

where the dots are part of the formula, punctuation marks may be, and frequently are, omitted.

Chemical symbols are not spaced:

$$Cr(N_2H_5)_2(SO_4)_2.$$

In printing numbers up to 9999 the figures should be set close up without a comma. In numbers above this, thin spaces should be used instead of commas: 1 000 000. (See also p. 16.)

More comprehensive recommendations are to be found in *The Printing of Mathematics* (Oxford, 1957). For a full treatment of the problems of printing chemical names and formulae, see the *Handbook for Chemical Society Authors*, Special Publication No. 14 (The Chemical Society, 1960).

SPACING

SPACING must be even. Paragraphs are not to be widely spaced for the sake of making break-lines. The spacing of break-lines should be normal. In general, close spacing is to be preferred, with the space of the line after a full point; but this must be regulated according to the class of work.

Break-lines should consist of more than five letters, except in narrow measures.

Poetry should not be more than thick-spaced.

If possible, avoid (especially in full measures) printing at the ends of lines—a, l., ll., p., *or* pp.

Do not divide initials: W. E. | Gladstone *not* W. | E. Gladstone.

Abbreviations of titles, such as M.P., D.D., M.A., or of occupations or parties, such as I.C.S., I.L.P., to have no space between the letters.

When titles of books or journals are represented by initials no space is to be put between the letters; **e.g.** *S.B.E.*, *J.T.S.* (and *Cal. S.P. Dom.*).

The spacing of references is to be as follows:

4 n.; 5 f.; 6 sq.: thin space (5 units) to precede n., f., sq.

4 n. 5; 5 et seq.; 12 and n. 7; p. 15 n. 3: ordinary space of line.

No spaces to be placed between lower-case abbreviations, as in e.g., i.e., q.v.

Indention of first lines of paragraphs to be generally one em for full measures. Sub-indention should be proportionate: the rule for all indention is not to drive too far in.

SPECIAL SIGNS AND SYMBOLS

THE signs + (plus), − (minus), = (equal to), > ('larger than', in etymology signifying 'gives' or 'has given'), < ('smaller than', in etymology signifying 'derived from') are often used in printing biological and philological works, and not only in those which are mathematical or arithmetical.

In such instances +, −, =, >, < should in the matter of spacing be treated as words are treated. For instance, in

spectabilis, *Bœrl. l.c.* (= Haasia spectabilis)

the = belongs to 'spectabilis' as much as to 'Haasia', and the sign should not be put close to 'Haasia'. A thin space only should be used.

In philological works an asterisk * prefixed to a word signifies a reconstructed form; a dagger † signifies an obsolete word. The latter sign, placed before a person's name, signifies deceased.

In early medical books the formulae were set in lower-case letters, j being used for i both singly and in the final letter, e.g. gr. j (one grain), ʒviij (eight ounces), ʒiij (three drachms), ℈iij (three scruples), ℳiiij (four minims).

THORN, ETH, WYN, YOGH

IN the printing of Old English follow copy for the use of thorn (þ, capital Þ) and eth (ð, capital Ð). The combination *th* is rare in Old English and should be avoided unless specified by the author (e.g. in 'diplomatic' texts).

Except in special circumstances—e.g. in the few early Middle English works in which both *w* and wyn are used—*w* is normally to be substituted for the wyn (ƿ) of the manuscript. Similarly, in Old English works print *g*, not ᵹ, except in the few works in which both letter-shapes occur.

In some early Middle English texts ᵹ is permissible, but normally ȝ is to be used for yogh in all Middle English work.

VOWEL-LIGATURES[1] (Æ AND Œ)

THE combinations *ae* and *oe* should each be printed as two letters in Latin and Greek words, e.g. Aeneid, Aeschylus, Caesar, Oedipus, Phoenicia; and in English, as formulae, phoenix. Print, e.g., oestrogen (where *oe* represents a single sound), but, e.g., chloro-ethane (not chloroethane) to avoid confusion.

In Old English words use the ligature Æ, æ, as Ælfric, Cædmon; and in French words use the ligature œ, as manœuvre.

---

[1] The separately written *oe, ae* are 'digraphs', because the sounds they represent are in modern pronunciation *not* diphthongs, though they were such in classical Latin; but *ch, ph, sh* are also digraphs. Æ, æ, Œ, œ, are rather single letters than digraphs, though they might be called ligatured digraphs.

SPELLINGS

ALTERNATIVE AND DIFFICULT SPELLINGS

abetter
abettor (*law*)
accepter (-or *in
  law and science*)
accommodation
adapter
adviser
ageing
align, -ment[1]
almanac[2]
ambidextrous
annex (*verb*)
annexe (*noun*)
apanage
apostasy
arcing[3]
artefact
aught (*anything*)[4]
ay (*yes*; pl. *the
  ayes have it*)
aye (*always*)
balk (*verb*)

bandoleer
bark (*ship*)
baulk (*timber*)
bivouac
bivouacked
bluish
bogey (*golf*)
bogie (*truck*),
  pl. -ies
bogy (*apparition*),
  pl. -ies
brier
brooch
  (*ornament*)
by and by
by the by
bye (*cricket*)
calendar, *n. and
  v.* (*register*)
calender, *n. and
  v.* (*press*)
canvas, *n.* (*cloth*)

canvas, *v.* (*past
  canvased,
  covered with
  canvas*)
canvass, *n. and v.*
  (*past canvassed
  (political*))
carcass, -es
censer (*vessel*)
censor (*official*)
centigramme
centred, -ing
cheque (*bank*)
chequered
  (*career*)
cider
cinematograph[5]
clench (*fists*)
clinch (*argument,
  nail*)
clue (*but clew for
  part of a sail*)

[1] This is the prevailing spelling: *O.E.D.* prefers alinement.
[2] But the *k* is retained in the *Oxford Almanack*.
[3] 'In derivatives formed from words ending in *c*, by adding a termination beginning with *e*, *i*, or *y*, the letter *k* is inserted after the *c*, in order that the latter may not be inaccurately pronounced like *s* before the following vowel.' (WEBSTER.) Electrical engineers, however, prefer arcing.
[4] Not ought.
[5] Usage favours this non-etymological form.

commitment
computer
conjurer
conjuror (*law*)
connection
consensus
conterminous
convection
convener
cony
copier
cornelian
corslet
cotillion
cottar (*peasant*)
cotter (*pin*)
coulter
crenellate
crosier
cryptogam (*bot.*)
cryptogram
  (*code*)
curb (*restrain*)
curtsy
defecate, -ation
deflexion
dependant
  (*noun*)
dependent
  (*adj.*)
depositary
  (*person*)
depository
  (*place*)
descendant
desiccate
develop, -ment

devest (*law*)[1]
dextrously
dike
disc
dispatch (*not
  despatch*)
draft (*prepare*)
draftsman (*one
  who drafts
  documents*)
draught (*of air*)
draughtsman
  (*one who draws*)
draughtsmen (*in
  game*)
drier (*machine*)
duffel
duress
dyeing (*cloth*)
ecology
ecstasy
educationist
embarrassment
embed
enclose[2]
encrust[3]
encyclopedia
endorse
enrol
ensure (*make
  safe*)
envelop (*verb*)
envelope (*noun*)
erector
faecal, faeces
felspar
fetid

flyer
foetal
foetus
fogy, *pl.* -ies
forbade
forbear (*abstain*)
forebear
  (*ancestor*)
foregone (*gone
  before*)
forestall
foretell
forgather
forgo
forme (*printer's*)
fount (*type*)
fulfil
fullness
fungous (*adj.*)
fungus (*noun*)
further[4]
fusilier
fusillade
gage (*pledge*)
gaol
gaoler
gauge (*measure*)
genuflexion
gibe
gillie
gipsy
glycerine
gormless
graminivorous
gramme
grammetre
gramophone

---

[1] Devest only, the intransitive form; divest, the transitive.
[2] But always inclosure of common lands, Inclosure Acts, etc.
[3] But incrustation.
[4] Some authors, however, still prefer farther (and also *superl.*, farthest).

grandad
grandam
granddaughter
granter (*one who grants*)
grantor (*in law: one who makes a grant*)
grey
grisly (*terrible*)
grizzly (*grey*)
grizzly bear
guerrilla
guild (*noun*)
haematite
haematology
haemorrhage
haemorrhoids
hairbreadth[1]
halberd
hallelujah
hallo
harass
hauler
haulm
hearken
hectogramme
hectolitre
hectometre
hiccup
Hindu
honorific
horsy
humous (*adj.*)
humus (*noun*)
idiosyncrasy
impinging
impostor
inflexion

inquire, inquiry
install
instalment
instil
insure (*in a society*)
inure
investor
inweave
jalopy
jam, v. (*not jamb*)
jamb (*of door*)
janizary
jews' harp(s)
judgement[2]
jugful
kerb (*pavement*)
kilogramme
kilogrammetre
kilolitre
kilometre
knick-knack
koala
Koran
lachrymose
lackey
lacquer
largess
lateish
leger line (*mus.*)
licence (*noun*)
license (*verb*)
licensee
Linnaean[3]
liquefy
liquorice
loadstone
loath (*adj.*)

loathe (*verb*)
lodestar
lour (*frown*)
lych-gate
macintosh
maharaja
mama (*mother*)
mandolin
manikin (*little man*)
mannequin (*model*)
marijuana
marquis
mayst
medieval
mightest
millepede
milligramme, -metre
milometer
mizen, -mast
moneyed
moneys
mongoose(s)
mortgagor
mould, -ing (*verb and noun*)
moustache
mucous (*adj.*)
mucus (*noun*)
Muhammad
Muslim
naught (*nothing*)
nerve-racking
net (*profits*)
nought (*zero*)
noviciate
nursling

---

[1] Some authors may prefer hair's breadth for emphasis.
[2] But judgment in legal works by legal authors.
[3] But Linnean Society.

octet
omelet
ouzel
overalls
oyez!
pacifist, -ism[1]
palaeography
Panjab
paraffin
parakeet
partisan
pasha
pastille
paviour
pendant (*noun*)
pendent (*adj.*)
peony
pewit
philosophers'
  stone (*not* -r's)
picnicking
podzolization
postilion
pott (*size of
  paper*)
practice (*noun*)
practise (*verb*)
premises
  (*no sing.,
  conveyancing*)
premiss, pre-
  misses (*logic*)
primeval

principle (*cf.
  principal*)
printer's error,
  pl. printer's *or*
  printers' errors[2]
programme
proletariat
propellant
  (*noun*)
propellent (*adj.*)
prophecy (*noun*)
prophesy (*verb*)
putrefy
pygmy
pyjamas
quartet, quintet
questionnaire
queuing
racket (*bat*)
rackets (*game*)
radical
  (*chemistry*)
radicle (*botany*)
ragee (*grain*)
raja
rarefaction, rarefy
rase (*erase*)
raze (*to the
  ground*)
recompense
  (*verb and noun*)
reflection
rhyme (*verse*)

rigors (*med.*)
rigour
rime (*hoar-frost*)
rodomontade
salvage (*of ship*)
savanna
scallop
selvage (*of cloth*)
sergeant
  (*military*)[3]
serjeant (*law*)
settlor (*in law*)]
Shakespeare
Shakespearian,
  -iana
show (*verb and
  noun*)[4]
sibyl, -line
silvan
silviculture
singeing
Sinhalese
skiing
speleology
stanch (*stop flow*)
stationary (*at rest*)
stationery (*paper*)
staunch (*true*)
steadfast
storey (*of house*)
superintendent
swingeing (*blow*)
sycamore[5]

---

[1] These short forms seem to be preferred to the longer and etymologically correct pacificist, pacificism. Print as above, unless otherwise directed.

[2] Where there is any ambiguity a hyphen may be used, as bad printers'-errors.

[3] But -*j*- in official Army Lists, etc.

[4] The spelling shew is founded on wrong etymology.

[5] A member of the maple (*Acer*) genus. The sycamine and the sycomore of the Bible are different trees.

tallness[1]
taxiing
teed (*golf*)
timpani (*pl. of* timpano)
tingeing
tiro
tocsin (*alarm bell*)
toxin (*poison*)

tranship, -ment
tsar
tympana (*pl. of* tympanum)
tyre[2]
veld
vendor[3]
veranda
vermilion

visor
wagon
whisky[4]
Whit Sunday
whitish
wistaria
wooed, woos
wrack (*sea-wrack*)

DOUBLING CONSONANTS WITH SUFFIXES

WORDS of one syllable, ending with one consonant preceded by one vowel, double that consonant on adding -*ed* or -*ing*:

beg	begged	begging
clap	clapped	clapping
fit	fitted	fitting
stop	stopped	stopping

Words of more than one syllable, ending with one consonant preceded by one vowel, and accented on the last syllable, double that consonant on adding -*ed* or -*ing*:

allot	allotted	allotting
commit	committed	committing
infer	inferred	inferring
occur	occurred	occurring
omit	omitted	omitting
prefer	preferred	preferring
trepan	trepanned	trepanning

[1] It is generally agreed that words ending in -*ll* should drop one *l* before -*less* and -*ly*; but there is not the same agreement in dropping an *l* before -*ness*.

[2] Although tire is correct etymology.

[3] The form vender is occasionally used.

[4] But note whiskey (Irish).

But words of this class, *not* accented on the last syllable, *do not double the last consonant*[1] on adding *-ed* or *-ing* or *-y*:

balloted, -ing
banqueted, -ing
bayoneted, -ing
benefited, -ing
biased, -ing
bigoted
billeted, -ing
bishoped, -ing
blanketed, -ing
bonneted, -ing
bracketed, -ing
budgeted, -ing
buffeted, -ing
carpeted, -ing
chirruped, -ing
combated, -ing
cricketing
crotcheted,
  -ing, -y

discomfited,
  -ing
docketed, -ing
faceted, -ing
ferreted, -ing
fidgeted, -ing, -y
filleted, -ing
filliped, -ing
focused, -ing
galloped, -ing
gibbeted, -ing
gossiped, -ing, -y
helmeted
jacketed, -ing
junketed, -ing
lettered, -ing
marketed, -ing
offered, -ing
packeted, -ing

paralleled,
  -ing[2]
picketed, -ing
pivoted, -ing
proffered, -ing
profited, -ing
rabbeted, -ing
rabbiting
rickety
ricocheted, -ing
riveted, -ing
russeted, -ing, -y
scalloped, -ing
trinketed, -ing
trousered, -ing
trumpeted, -ing
visited, -ing
wainscoted,
  -ing

In words ending in *-l* the final consonant is generally doubled,[3] whether accented on the last syllable or not:

annulled, -ing
appalled, -ing
apparelled, -ing
bevelled, -ing
channelled, -ing
chiselled, -ing
compelled, -ing
counselled, -ing
cudgelled, -ing
dishevelled, -ing
empanelled, -ing

enrolled, -ing
extolled, -ing
fulfilled, -ing
grovelled, -ing
impelled, -ing
initialled, -ing
instilled, -ing
kennelled, -ing
labelled, -ing
levelled, -ing
libelled, -ing

marshalled, -ing
modelled, -ing
panelled, -ing
parcelled, -ing
quarrelled, -ing
revelled, -ing
rivalled, -ing
shovelled, -ing
trammelled, -ing
travelled, -ing
tunnelled, -ing

[1] But note words ending in *-l* and also worshipped, -er, -ing.

[2] This is an exception to the rule relating to the doubling of *l*.

[3] But appealed, -ing; travailed, -ing; etc.

FIFTEENTH- TO SEVENTEENTH-CENTURY WORKS

WHEN it is necessary to reproduce the spellings and printed forms of old writers the following rules should be observed:

Initial *u* is printed *v*, as in vnderstande. Also in such combinations as wherevpon.

Medial *v* is printed *u*, as in haue, euer.[1]

Initial and medial *j* are printed *i*, as in iealousie, iniurie, but in roman numerals *j* may be used finally, as viij.

In capitals the U is non-existent, and should always be printed with a V, initially and medially, as VNIVERSITY.

In yᵉ and yᵗ the second letter should be a superior, and without a full point.

FORMATION OF PLURALS IN ENGLISH

WORDS ENDING IN -E AND -Y

PLURALS of nouns ending in *-e* are formed by adding *-s*; e.g. divergence, divergences; excellence, excellences.

Nouns ending in *-y* preceded by a consonant form their plurals by changing *y* into *ies*; e.g. his Excellency, their Excellencies; ruby, rubies; story, stories. An exception is found in fly (a carriage), *pl.* flys. Proper names also retain *y*; e.g. the Carys, the Merrys, the three Marys.

---

[1] Old manuscripts, however, are often inconsistent in the use of *u* and *v*, and where exact reproduction is needed the copy must be followed.

WORDS ENDING IN -O

The plurals of nouns ending in -o are often confusing, owing to the absence of any settled system. The following is a list of common words with this ending, showing preferred spellings:

albinos	egos	octavos
altos	electros	oratorios
archipelagos	embargoes	peccadilloes
armadillos	embryos	photos
banjos	Eskimos	pianos
bastinados	fiascos	piccolos
boleros	flamingos	placebos
bravoes (*hired*)	folios	porticoes
bravos (*of the crowd*)	frescoes	potatoes
buffaloes	ghettos	provisos
calicoes	gringos	punctilios
cantos	grottoes	quartos
cargoes	haloes	radios
centos	heroes	ratios
chromos	impresarios	salvoes
commandos	innuendoes	scenarios
concertos	kilos	solos[1]
crescendos	lassoes	sopranos
curios	librettos	stilettos
dados	Lotharios	stuccoes
dagos	magnetos	tiros
dingoes	mangoes	tomatoes
dodos	manifestos	tornadoes
dominoes	mementoes	torpedoes
duodecimos	memos	torsos
dynamos	mosquitoes	vetoes
echoes	mottoes	volcanoes
	Negroes	zeros

COMPOUNDS

Compound words formed by a noun and an adjective, or by two nouns connected by a preposition, form their plurals by a change in the chief word; e.g.

[1] But soli when used as a purely musical term.

adjutants-general, aides-de-camp, courts martial, cousins-german, fleurs-de-lis, men-of-war, poets-laureate, sons-in-law.

Note that the singular form is used with a plural number in such combinations as: an eight-foot stone, a seven-inch gun, a six-mile track, a twelve-pound shot.

FORMATION OF PLURALS IN WORDS OF FOREIGN ORIGIN

PLURALS of nouns taken into English from other languages sometimes follow the laws of inflexion of those languages. But often, in non-technical works, additional forms are used, constructed after the English manner. Print as below unless instructed otherwise.

Singular	Plural
addendum	addenda[1]
——	agenda
alga	algae
alkali	alkalis
alumnus	alumni
amanuensis	amanuenses
analysis	analyses
animalculum	animalcula
antithesis	antitheses
apex	apexes
aphis	aphides[2]
apparatus	apparatuses
appendix	appendices[3]
arcanum	arcana
atrium	atria *or* atriums
automaton	automatons[4]
axis	axes

[1] See reference to this word on p. 15.

[2] Of unknown etymology; aphid, *pl.* aphids, is also common.

[3] Appendixes, once common, is dropping out of use.

[4] But automata when used collectively.

Singular	*Plural*
bacillus	bacilli
bandit	bandits
basis	bases
beau	beaux
broccoli	broccolis
bronchus	bronchi
bureau	bureaux
cactus	cacti
calculus	calculi
calix	calices
chateau	chateaux
chrysalis	chrysalises
coagulum	coagula
corrigendum	corrigenda[1]
cortex	cortices
crematorium	crematoria
crisis	crises
criterion	criteria
crux	cruces
curriculum	curricula
datum	data
desideratum	desiderata
dilettante	dilettantes *or* dilettanti
effluvium	effluvia
elenchus	elenchi
ellipsis	ellipses
encomium	encomiums
ephemera	ephemerae
epithalamium	epithalamia
equinox	equinoxes
erratum	errata[1]
focus	focuses[2] (*familiar*)
formula	formulas[2]
fungus	fungi
genius (*person*)	geniuses[3] (*persons*)

[1] See reference to these words on p. 15.

[2] But some words should retain their Latin plurals in their scientific sense: foci, formulae, indices, media. Also in 'mass media'.

[3] Genie, in the sense of a tutelary spirit, must have the plural genii.

Singular	Plural
genus	genera
gladiolus	gladioli
gymnasium	gymnasiums
helix	helices
hiatus	hiatuses
hypothesis	hypotheses
ignis fatuus	ignes fatui
ignoramus	ignoramuses
index	indexes[1]
iris	irises
lacuna	lacunas or lacunae
lamina	laminae
larva	larvae
lemma	lemmas[2]
maestro	maestri
matrix	matrices
mausoleum	mausoleums[3]
maximum	maxima
medium	mediums[1] (*fam.*)
memorandum	memorandums[4]
metamorphosis	metamorphoses
miasma	miasmata
minimum	minima
narcissus	narcissi
nebula	nebulae
nucleus	nuclei
oasis	oases
octopus	octopuses
papilla	papillae
parenthesis	parentheses
parhelion	parhelia
phenomenon	phenomena
plateau	plateaux
postscript	postscripts
radius	radii
radix	radices

[1] See p. 68 n. 2.
[2] But lemmata in botany, embryology, and lexicography.
[3] Mausolea is also used.
[4] Memorandums, meaning separate notes, but in a collective or special sense we must print memoranda.

Singular	*Plural*
ranunculus	ranunculuses[1]
sanatorium	sanatoriums
scholium	scholia
series	series
spectrum	spectra
speculum	specula
stamen	stamens
stimulus	stimuli
stratum	strata
syllabus	syllabuses
synopsis	synopses
tableau	tableaux
terminus	termini
thesis	theses
ultimatum	ultimatums[2]
virtuoso	virtuosi
virus	viruses
vortex	vortexes (*fam.*)

HYPHENED AND NON-HYPHENED WORDS[3]

THE hyphen need not, as a rule, be used to join an adverb to the adjective it qualifies, e.g. a beautifully furnished house. But where the adverb might not at once be recognized as such, use the hyphen, e.g. a well-known statesman, an ill-educated man, a new-found country, the best-known proverb, a good-sized room.

[1] But print ranunculi if consistently so in the copy.
[2] Ultimata is also used.
[3] See *O.E.D.*, vol. i, p. xxxiii, art. 'Combinations', where Sir James Murray writes: 'In many combinations the hyphen becomes an expression of this unification of sense. When this unification and specialization has proceeded so far that we no longer analyse the combination into its elements, but take it in as a whole, as in *blackberry*, *postman*, *newspaper*, pronouncing it in speech with a single accent, the hyphen is usually omitted, and the fully developed compound is written as a single word. But as this also is a question of degree, there are necessarily many compounds as to which usage has not yet determined

Where an adverb qualifies a predicate, the hyphen *should not* be used, e.g. this fact is well known.

Where either (1) a noun and an adjective or a participle, or (2) an adjective and a noun, in combination, are used as a compound adjective, the hyphen *should* be used, e.g. a poverty-stricken family, a blood-red hand, an early nineteenth-century invention. So, too, adjectival combinations of colours, e.g. a bluish-grey haze (but . . . was bluish grey). For the use of hyphens in fractions see p. 16.

A compound noun which has *but one accent*, and from familiar use has become one word, requires no hyphen. Examples:

bláckbird	dústman	fóotprint

Many words in common use, originally printed as two words or hyphenated, are now used without the hyphen. Examples:

aerofoil	battlefield	candlepower
amidships	bedroom	casework
antenatal	bedsore	catchword
antitetanus	bookwork	centigrade
antitoxin	breakdown	centimetre
anybody	breakup	centrifugal
anyhow	brickwork	childbirth
anyone[1]	bygone	coalfield
anything	byname	coaxial
anywhere	bypass	coeducation
armchair	bypath	coeval
background	byword	coexistence

whether they are to be written with the hyphen or as single words.'

And again, in *The Schoolmasters' Year-book* for 1903, Sir James Murray writes: 'There is no rule, propriety, or consensus of usage in English for the use or absence of the hyphen, except in cases where grammar or sense is concerned; as in a day well remembered, but a well-remembered day, the sea of a deep green, a deep-green sea, a baby little expected, a little-expected baby, not a deep green sea, a little expected baby.'

[1] In the sense anybody, everybody, etc., but any one, every one, some one, each with two accents, in other uses.

coextensive
cornfield
cosecant
cosine
cotangent
countryside
crossword
  (*puzzle*)
curvilinear
decibel
disyllable
downhill
electrolyte
electromotive
electrostatic
endpaper
evermore
everyday
  (*as adj.*)
everyone[1]
everything
everyway (*adv.*)
eyewitness
fairyland
farmyard
fatstock
feedback
filmsetting
flashback
flashpoint
flyleaf
flysheet
flywheel
folklore
foodstuffs
footnote
footsore
footstool
freeboard
freshwater
  (*as adj.*)

godlike
goodwill
grassland
grindstone
halftone
hallmark
handbook
handlist
headmaster
headquarters
heartbeat
heyday
hillside
hilltop
hopscotch
horsepower
horseshoe
hundredweight
indiarubber
interrelationship
keynote
kilogramme
kilometre
ladybird
ladylike
lawcourt[2]
lawsuit
layout
letterhead
lifelike
lifelong
lifetime
livestock
maybe
megawatt
microfilm
midbrain
midday
midline
milestone
milligramme

millimetre
miscall
monochrome
motherland
motorway
multiracial
newcomer
newfangled
noonday
notebook
offprint
offshoot
onrush
outdoor
overleaf
overnight
  (*adj. & adv.*)
paperback
particoloured
peacetime
percentage
polyethylene
polyvinyl
postcard
postnatal
pressman
radioactive
rainfall
reappear
reappraisal
reimburse
reinstate
reopen
reprint
runoff
runway
screenplay
seaplane
seaside
seaweed
selfsame

---

[1] See p. 71 n. 1.   [2] But the Law Courts.

sidelight	superscript	unselfconscious
smallpox	supranormal	wartime
someone[1]	teenager	watercourse
stepfather	terracotta	wavelength
stockpile	textbook	wellnigh
subcommittee	thermonuclear	worthwhile
subscript	today	(*attrib.*)
subway	tomorrow	wrongdoing
suchlike	tonight	wryneck
supermarket	twofold	zigzag

Many compound words with more than one stress, e.g. cróss-quéstion, eásy-góing, shórt-térm, require hyphens. A hyphen is also usually desirable in compounds of which the first element ends with a vowel and the second element begins with a vowel, e.g. aero-elastic, radio-isotope, sea-urchin, not aeroelastic, radioisotope, seaurchin; or where the first element ends with the same consonant as that beginning the second element, e.g. part-time.[2]

Examples:[3]

aide-de-camp	birth-rate	by-play
air-blast	bi-weekly	by-plot
air-to-air	blood-pressure	by-product
amino-acids[4]	blood-stream	by-road
ante-mortem	blood-supply	by-way
(*adj.*)	body-weight	cat's-paw
anti-freeze	boiler-room	change-over
Attorney-General	boiling-point	chock-full
arrow-head	by-election	common-sense
bench-mark	by-lane	(*as adj.*)
bile-duct	by-law	co-operate

[1] See p. 71 n. 1.
[2] These rules do not apply to words of great frequency: thus coeducation and radioactive are normally now printed without hyphens, but until recently required hyphens.
[3] The hyphen may be dropped in many of these words when used attributively: thus arrowhead formation (but 'the arrow-head is poisoned'); firsthand information (but 'that information is first-hand').
[4] Although some editors prefer amino acids in scientific work.

co-ordinate[1]
count-down
cross-section
death-rate
de-ice
ding-dong
drip-proof
ear-rings
engine-room
eye-muscles
fall-out
far-fetched
filter-paper
first-hand
freezing-point
gall-bladder
get-at-able
good-bye
good-day
good-night
ground-level
guide-book
gutta-percha
half-crown
half-dozen
half-hour
half-past
half-title
half-way
  (*adj. & adv.*)
head-dress
head-note

heat-content
hip-joint
hoar-frost
hymn-book
infra-red
jaw-bone
knick-knack
know-how
lady-in-waiting
lamb's-wool
lay-by
lead-pencil
looking-glass
look-out
loud-speaker
Major-General
man-of-war
melting-point
micro-organisms
mis-spelling
near-by
  (*adj.*)
nerve-cells
non-co-operation
non-toxic
off-hand
oft-times
out-and-out
out-of-date[2]
out-of-doors
over-all (*adj.*)
physico-chemical

post-mortem
  (*adj. & noun*)
pre-eminent
pulse-rate
race-course
re-bound[3] (*as
  a book*)
re-cover[3] (*a
  chair*)
re-enter
re-entrant
re-form[3] (*form
  again*)
re-sell, -sale
sea-breeze
second-hand
set-back
short-circuit
  (*verb*)
son-in-law
spear-head
starting-point
sub-title
swing-wing
  (*aircraft*)
table-land
take-off
take-over
test-tube
title-page
topsy-turvy
turning-point

[1] Usually one word in mathematical works; note also uncoordinate.

[2] As, out-of-date (or up-to-date) records; but print 'the records are out of date', etc.

[3] 'The hyphen is often used when a writer wishes to mark the fact that he is using not a well-known compound verb, but *re-* as a living prefix attached to a simple verb (*re-pair* = pair again); also usually before *e* (*re-emerge*), and sometimes before other vowels (*re-assure*, usually *reassure*); also when the idea of repetition is to be emphasized, especially in such phrases as *make and re-make*.' (*Concise Oxford Dictionary*, p. 1025.)

twin-screw	vice-consul	water-line
ultra-violet	volt-ampere	web-offset
up-country	water-colour	well-being
up-to-date[1]	water-level	year-book[2]

Half an inch, half a dozen, etc., require no hyphens. Print also without hyphens:

beta ray	good humour	post office
blood bank	good nature	press reader
blood count	heat flow	radium therapy
blood group	high priest	revenue office
brake horsepower	high road	Reynolds numbers
cast iron	ill health	*(no apostrophe)*
coat of arms	ill humour	right angle
common sense	ill luck	screw thread
(adj. & noun	ill nature	sheet iron
together)	ill will	short circuit
court martial	in so far	*(noun)*
dare say	mother tongue	square root
decimal point	motor car	stop valve
easy chair	near by *(adv.)*	stress rate
fellow men, etc.	nickel silver	sweepback angle
flow rate	none the less	two and six
foot candle	no one	*(in money)*
for ever	Notary Public	twopence
free will	on to	halfpenny
(but freewill	over all *(adv.)*	Union Jack
offering)	per cent	worth while
gamma ray	plum pudding	*(predic.)*
gas poisoning	*post mortem (adv.)*	yield point

WORDS ENDING IN -ABLE

WORDS ending in silent *e* generally lose the *e* when *-able* is added:

adorable	desirable	indispensable
arguable	excusable	pleasurable

But this rule is open to exceptions upon which authorities are not agreed. The following spellings, with or without the *e*, are to be followed:

advisable	excisable	palatable
analysable	excitable	partakable
ascribable	finable	persuadable
atonable	forgivable	provable
believable	framable	rateable
blameable	giveable	receivable
bribable	hireable	reconcilable
conceivable	immovable	removable
confinable	improvable	reputable
consolable	incurable	saleable
conversable	indescribable	sizeable
creatable	inflatable	solvable
datable	irreconcilable	statutable
debatable	likeable	storable
declinable	linable	tameable
definable	liveable	translatable
dilatable	losable	tuneable
dissolvable	lovable	unmistakable
drivable	malleable	unscalable
durable	measurable	unshakeable
endorsable	movable[1]	usable
evadable	nameable	

If *-able* is added to a word which in its simplest form ends in *y*, this *y* usually changes to *i* :[2]

dutiable	leviable	reliable
justifiable	rectifiable	undeniable

In words ending in *ce* or *ge*, the *e* should be retained to preserve the soft sound of *c* or *g*:

bridgeable	knowledgeable	peaceable
changeable	manageable	pronounceable
chargeable	marriageable	serviceable
irreplaceable	noticeable	traceable

[1] In legal works moveable.
[2] But flyable, buyable, employable.

Many verbs ending in *-ate* drop this ending in the derivative adjectives in *-able*:[1]

abominable	delineable	expiable
alienable	demonstrable	penetrable
appreciable	educable	permeable
calculable	execrable	superannuable

Words ending in double *e* retain both letters:

agreeable	feeable	foreseeable

In words of English formation, a final consonant is usually doubled before *-able* when doubled in the present participle:

admittable	deferrable[2]	incurrable
biddable	demurrable	rebuttable
clubbable	forgettable	regrettable
conferrable	gettable	

Other examples of words ending in *-able*:

actionable	illimitable	mutable
adaptable	immutable	objectionable
administrable	impalpable	obtainable
amiable	impassable (*not*	perishable
assessable	*to be passed*)	readable
available	impeccable	registrable
bearable	imperturbable	retractable
capable	implacable	suitable
comfortable	indefatigable	tolerable
despicable	indubitable	transferable
developable	inimitable	unconscionable
eatable	irrefragable	unexceptionable
equable	laughable	un-get-at-able
expendable	manœuvrable	unknowable

[1] But *-at* is retained when the verb is disyllabic, as creatable, dictatable.

[2] But inferable (against inferring), preferable (preferring), referable (referring), transferable (transferring); contrast insufferable (suffering), marketable (marketing).

WORDS ENDING IN -IBLE

WORDS ending in *-able* are derived from several sources, including:

(i) Latin suffix *-abilis* added to Latin roots, e.g. indubitable from *dubito*, 'I doubt';

(ii) Latin, through French, e.g. amiable from French *aimable*, from Latin *amabilis*, from *amo*, 'I love';

(iii) *-able* as an English suffix added to English words or roots; lovable, taxable, un-get-at-able.

The ending *-ible* is used only 'whenever there was or might be a Latin *-ibilis*' and not 'for words of distinctly French or English origin' (*O.E.D.* s.v. *-ble*).

Examples:

accessible	divisible	intangible
adducible	extendible	irascible
avertible	flexible	irresistible
collapsible	gullible	legible
comprehensible	impassible	persuasible
contemptible	(*unfeeling*)	reversible
defensible	indelible	susceptible
discernible	indigestible	vendible

WORDS ENDING IN -IZE, -ISE, AND -YSE

THE *-ize*, not *-ise*, ending should be used where both spellings are in use. Generally, *-ize* is a suffix applied to the stems of nouns ending in *-ism*, *-ization*, *-izer*, *-y*, or to the complete noun.

Examples:

agony	agonize	civilization	civilize
appetizer	appetize	criticism	criticize
canal	canalize	transistor	transistorize

The ending *-ise* is correct when the noun has *-is-* as part of the stem, e.g. in the syllables *-vis-* (seeing), *-cis-* (cutting), *-mis-* (putting), and is also used for those nouns which do not terminate in *-ism*, *-ization*, etc. Exceptions are aggrandizement/aggrandize, recognition/recognize, and others noted in *C.O.D.* as 'assimilated to verbs in -ize'. Reference should be made to *C.O.D.* and Collins, *Authors' and Printers' Dictionary*, if there is any doubt. Some of the more common *-ise* words follow:

advertise	disguise	misadvise
advise	emprise	premise
apprise	enterprise	prise (open)
chastise	excise	reprise
circumcise	exercise	revise
comprise	expertise	supervise
compromise	franchise	surmise
demise	improvise	surprise
despise	incise	televise
devise	merchandise	treatise

In words such as analyse, catalyse, paralyse, *-lys-* is part of the Greek and not a suffix like *-ize*. There is therefore no parallel with *-ize* words, and consequently the spelling *-yze* is etymologically incorrect, and not to be used—except when following American printing style.

WORDS ENDING IN -MENT

IN words ending in *-ment* print the *e* when it occurs in the verbal form, as abridgement, acknowledgement, judgement,[1] lodgement.[2] But omit the *e* in development, envelopment, in accordance with the spelling of the verbal forms develop, envelop.

[1] But judgment in legal works by legal authors.

[2] 'I protest against the unscholarly habit of omitting it from "abridgement", "acknowledgement", "judgement", "lodgement",—which is against all analogy, etymology, and orthoepy, since elsewhere *g* is hard in English when not followed by *e* or *i*. I think the University Press ought to set a scholarly example, instead of following the ignorant to do ill, for the sake of saving four *e*'s. The word "judgement" has been spelt in the Revised Version correctly.' (Sir James Murray.)

DECIMAL CURRENCY

IN British decimal currency, introduced on 15 February 1971, sums of money should be printed as follows:

Amounts in whole pounds are printed: £2,542

Amounts expressed in new pence: 56p (no point) *not* £0·56

Mixed amounts of pounds and new pence should be printed thus: £24·74 *not* £24·74p

The new halfpenny should be expressed as a fraction: £12·45½; 7½p

There must always be two figures after the decimal point: £15·50; £15·07

For a long period after the introduction of decimal currency amounts expressed in £ s. d. will continue to be found in 'copy', and this must be followed in the choice between £ s. d. and decimals, following the rules for each given in this book.

Amounts in £ s. d. will naturally be found in:

(*a*) resetting books published before 1971, including all classics, and literature generally;

(*b*) quotations in new books from works (including letters and documents) dating from before 1971;

(*c*) new books in which the author is referring in his own words to events and conditions before 1971; e.g. 'In 1969 income tax stood at 8s. 3d. in the £'; 'My aunt gave me 3s. 6d. to buy a story-book.'

In categories (*b*) and (*c*) and in annotated editions of (*a*) it will be for the author or editor to decide, in future years, whether to introduce decimal equivalents of pre-1971 amounts for the benefit of those to whom shillings and pence are unfamiliar, or for ease of comparison (e.g. in statistics) with post-1971 figures.

RULES FOR SETTING
FOREIGN LANGUAGES

FRENCH

In adding this section to the *Rules* (in the edition of 1904) Horace Hart acknowledged his debt to *Les Règles de la composition typographique, à l'usage des compositeurs, des correcteurs et des imprimeurs*, by Désiré Greffier. In revising them for this edition we have consulted the 'modificatif' of the *Règlement de composition typographique et de correction* of the Imprimerie nationale (*Orthographe technique* — J. 302705) and the *Code typographique* of the Syndicat national des Cadres et Maîtrises du Livre, de la Presse et des Industries graphiques (5th ed., 1954).

The Académie française is an official institution whose responsibility is to purify, standardize, clarify, and maintain the essential character of the French language through its *Dictionnaire* (eight editions, 1694–1935) and its *Grammaire*.

THE English printer called upon to set works in the French language will do well, first of all, to make a careful examination of some examples from the best French printing-offices. He will find that French printers act on rules differing in many points from the rules to which the English compositor is accustomed; but he will not be able to escape from his difficulties by the simple expedient of following the copy.

For works in the French language, such as textbooks for use in schools, the English printer may get reprint copy for text and manuscript for notes. It is, as a rule, safe for him to follow the reprint copy; but there is the difficulty that when the work forms part of a series it does not always happen that the reprint copy for one book corresponds in typographical style with reprint copy for other works in the same series. Hence he should apply himself to understand the following rules, and should hunt out examples of their application, so that they may remain in his memory.

Abbreviations

Such words as article, chapitre, scène, titre, figure, are abbreviated only when in parentheses, as references; in the text they are put in full. The word premier (*or* première) is spelt out following such nouns (and after acte): Article premier, Art. 2.

Saint, sainte, when they occur very often, as in religious works, may be abbreviated, taking a capital letter: S. Louis, Ste Marie. But this is never so in a surname or when they form part of a place-name, e.g. Saint-Germain-des-Prés; in which case Saint- and Sainte- take a capital and are followed by a hyphen.[1] (See also p. 87.)

Contractions such as St, Ste, Mme, Mlle, etc., do not take the full point, the rule being that the full point is not placed after a contraction when the last letter of the word and the last letter of the contraction are the same.

The words monsieur, messieurs, madame, mesdames, monseigneur, messeigneurs, mademoiselle, mesdemoiselles, are written in full and all in lower case when addressing a person: Oui, madame; Non, monsieur le duc; J'espère que monseigneur viendra;[2] J'ai vu monsieur votre père. In most other cases initial capitals are used: M. (for monsieur), Mme (for madame), Mgr (for monseigneur), etc. The words Sa Majesté, Son Éminence, Leurs Altesses, when followed by another title, are put as initials, thus S. M. l'Empereur; but not otherwise.

[1] St-Germain, Ste-Catherine, St-Hilaire, la St-Jean, l'église de St-Sulpice are, however, met with in gazetteers, guide-books, etc.

[2] But, when referring to a third person: ...que M. Berthelot...

The name Jésus-Christ is abbreviated only after a date, thus: 337 avant J.-C. This is sometimes printed 337 av. J.-C.

Other examples of abbreviations:

mn - minute

liv.	(livre)	etc.	(et cætera)
chap.	(chapitre)	c.-à-d.	(c'est-à-dire)
t.	(tome)	Cie, Cie	(compagnie)
d°	(dito)	Dr	(docteur)
f°	(folio)	M.	(monsieur)
in-f°	(in-folio)	Me, M^e	(maître)
in-8°	(in-octavo)	Mme, Mme	(madame)
in-4°	(in-quarto)	Mlle, Mlle	(mademoiselle)
ms.	(manuscrit)	MM.	(messieurs)
mss.	(manuscrits)	N.-S. J.-C.	(Notre-Seigneur
n°	(numéro)		Jésus-Christ)
p.	(page)	Cte	(comte)
p. *or* pp.	(pages)	Mis	(marquis)
P.-S.	(post-scriptum)	Vve	(veuve)
Ier		S. A.	(Son Altesse)
1er }	(premier)	LL. AA. II.	(Leurs **Alt**esses
Ier }			Impériales)
II, IIe, 2e (deuxième)			

Abbreviations of metric units:[1]

M	(méga = million)	a.	(are)
mam.	(myriamètre)	ca. *or* m^2	(centiare)
km.	(kilomètre)	das.	(décastère)
hm.	(hectomètre)	s. *or* m^3	(stère)
dam.	(décamètre)	ds.	(décistère)
m.	(mètre)	t.	(tonne)
dm.	(décimètre)	q.	(quintal métrique)
cm.	(centimètre)	kg.	(kilogramme)
mc. *or* m^3	(mètre cube)	hg.	(hectogramme)
mq. *or* m^2	(mètre carré)	dag.	(décagramme)
mm.	(millimètre)	g.	(gramme)
mmq. *or* mm^2	(millimètre	dg.	(décigramme)
	carré)	cg.	(centigramme)
mmc. *or* mm^3	(millimètre	mg.	(milligramme)
	cube)	kl.	(kilolitre)
ha.	(hectare)	hl.	(hectolitre)

[1] Full points are used in general work but omitted in scientific contexts.

dal.	(décalitre)	cl.	(centilitre)
l.	(litre)	ml.	(millilitre)
dl.	(décilitre)		

Put: 20 francs, 20 mètres, 20 litres, 20 milli-grammes. If, however, followed by fractions, then put: 20 fr. 50, or $20^{fr},50$; 20 m. 50, or $20^{m},50$; 20 l. 50, or $20^{l},50$.

The words kilogrammes, kilomètres, and kilo-grammètres, followed by fractions, are given thus: 50 kg. 3 or $50^{kg},3$; 5 km. 3 or $5^{km},3$; 2 kgm. 4 or $2^{kgm},4$.

In works crowded with figures, one can even put: $0^{m},5$ for 5 décimètres; $0^{m},15$ for 15 centimètres; $0^{m},008$ for 8 millimètres.

The cubic metre followed by a fraction is given thus: $4^{mc},005$ or $4^{m3},005$ ($= 4$ mètres cubes 5 millimètres cubes); the square metre thus: $4^{mq},05$ or $4^{m2},05$ ($= 4$ mètres carrés 5 centimètres carrés).

The French use a decimal comma instead of a decimal point: $2,3 = 2\cdot3$.

Per cent is generally put o/o, but pour 100, p. 100, and % are also used. In business letters pour cent is always pour % : à trente jours, 3 pour % d'escompte.

Accented capitals

With one exception accents are to be used with capital letters in French. The exception is the grave accent on the capital letter A in such lines as:

> A la porte de la maison, etc.;
>
> A cette époque, etc.;

and in display lines such as:

FÉCAMP A GENÈVE

MACHINES A VAPEUR

In these the preposition A takes no accent; but we must, to be correct, print Étienne, Étretat; and

DÉPÔT, ÉVÊQUE, PRÉVÔT in cap. lines.[1] Small capitals, where used, should be accented in the same way as large capitals.

Awkward divisions: abbreviated words and large numbers expressed in figures

One should avoid ending a line with an apostrophe, such as: Quoi qu' | il dise.

If a number expressed in figures is too long to be got into a line, or cannot be taken to the next without prejudice to the spacing, a part of the number should be put as a word, thus: 100 mil- | lions.

Capital and lower case

In the names of authors of the seventeenth century, which are preceded by an article, the latter should commence with a capital letter: La Fontaine, La Bruyère. Exceptions are names taken from the Italian, thus: le Tasse, le Dante, le Corrège.[2] As to names of persons, the usage of the individuals themselves should be adopted: de la Bruyère (his signature at the end of a letter), De la Fontaine (end of fable 'Le Lièvre et la Tortue'), Lamartine, Le Verrier, Maxime Du Camp. In place-names the article should have a lower-case initial: le Mans, le Havre, which the Académie[3] adopts; la Ferté, with no hyphen after the article, but connected by a hyphen with other place-names, as la Ferté-sous-Jouarre. It is advisable to consult, for example, *Petit Larousse* in each instance.

[1] There is no uniformity of practice in French printing-offices in regard to the accentuation of capital letters generally, although there is a consensus of opinion as to retaining accents for the letter E. The letter A, when a capital, standing for à, is never accented by French printers.

[2] Many now write 'Dante' for 'le Dante'. 'Tasse' is also met with for 'le Tasse'.

[3] The Académie française; see introductory note, p. 81.

Numbers of volumes, books, titles, acts of plays, the years of the Republican Calendar, are put in large capitals: an IV, acte V, tome VI; also numerals belonging to proper names: Louis XII; but the numbers of the arrondissements of Paris: le 15ᵉ arrondissement.

Numbers of scenes of plays, if there are no acts, are also put in full capitals: *Les Précieuses ridicules*, sc. V; also chapters if they form the principal division: *Joseph*, ch. VI. If, however, scenes of plays and chapters are secondary divisions, they are put in small capitals: *Le Cid*, acte I, sc. II; *Histoire de France*, liv. VI, ch. VII. The numbers of centuries are generally put in small capitals: au XIXᵉ (*or* XIXᵉᵐᵉ) siècle.

The first word of a title takes an initial capital letter: J'ai vu jouer *Les Femmes savantes*; on lit dans *Le Radical*. However, where an author prefers lower-case *l* for the definite article (*le, la, les*) beginning a title, this style should be adopted. If a substantive in a title immediately follows *Le, La, Les, Un, Une*, it is also given a capital letter, thus: *Les Précieuses ridicules*. If such substantive is preceded by an adjective, this also receives an initial capital letter: *La Folle Journée*; if, however, the adjective follows, it has a lower-case initial: *L'Âge ingrat*. If the title commences with any other word than *le, la, les, un, une*, or an adjective, the words following are all in lower case unless they are proper nouns: *De la terre à la lune*; *Sur la piste*.

In titles of fables and dramatic works names of the characters have capital initials: *Le Renard et les Raisins*; *Le Lion et le Rat*; *Marceau, ou les Enfants de la République*.

In catalogues or indexes having the first word(s) in parentheses after the noun commencing the line, the first word transposed has a capital letter: Homme (Faiblesse de l'); Honneur (L'); Niagara (Les Chutes du).

If the words in parentheses are part of the title of a work, the same rule is followed as to capitals as above given: *Héloïse* (*La Nouvelle*); *Mort* (*La Vie ou la*).

The words saint, sainte, when referring to the saints themselves, have, except when commencing a sentence, always lower-case initials: saint Louis, saint Paul, sainte Cécile. But when referring to place-names, feast-days, etc., capital letters and hyphens are used: Saint-Domingue, la Saint-Jean. (See also, as to abbreviations of saint, sainte, p. 82.)

I. Use capital letters as directed below:

(1) Words relating to God: le Seigneur, l'Être suprême, le Très-Haut, le Saint-Esprit.

(2) In enumerations, when each one commences a new line, a capital is put immediately after the ordinal figure:

> 1° L'Europe.
> 2° L'Asie, etc.

But when the enumeration is run on, lower-case letters are used: 1° l'Europe, 2° l'Asie, etc.

(3) Words representing abstract qualities personified: La Renommée ne vient souvent qu'après la Mort.

(4) The planets and constellations: la Terre, la Lune, Mars, le Bélier.

(5) Religious festivals: la Pentecôte.

(6) Historical events: la Révolution, la Réstauration, la Renaissance, l'Antiquité, la Réforme.

(7) The names of streets, squares, etc.: la rue des Mauvais-Garçons, la place de la Nation, la fontaine des Innocents.

(8) Names of public buildings, churches, etc.: l'Opéra, l'Odéon, Hôtel de Ville.

(9) Names relating to institutions, public bodies, religious, civil, or military orders (but only the word after the article): l'Académie française (but

la Comédie-Française, le Théâtre-Français, and la Comédie-Italienne), la Légion d'honneur, le Conservatoire de musique.

(10) Surnames and nicknames, without hyphens: Louis le Grand.

(11) Honorary titles: Son Éminence, Leurs Altesses. But cf. p. 82 *ad fin.* for use of lower case when addressing a person.

(12) Adjectives in geographical expressions: la mer Rouge, le golfe Persique.

(13) The names of the cardinal points designating an extent of territory: l'Amérique du Nord; aller dans le Midi. See II (2).

(14) The word Église when it denotes the Church as an institution: l'Église catholique; but when relating to a building put église.

(15) The word État when it designates the nation, the country: La France est un puissant État.

(16) Persons of a nation and ages: les Anglais, les Anciennes et les Modernes, les Français.

(17) Personal and geographical proper names.

(18) Adjectives joined by hyphens to preceding nouns: Comédie-Française, Comédie-Italienne.

II. Use lower-case initials for:

(1) The names of members of religious orders: un carme (a Carmelite), un templier (a Templar). But the names of the orders themselves take capitals: l'ordre des Templiers, des Carmes.

(2) The names of the cardinal points: le nord, le sud. But see I (13) above.

(3) Adjectives derived from proper names: la langue française, l'ère napoléonienne.

(4) Objects named from persons or places: un quinquet (an Argand lamp), un verre de champagne.

(5) Days of the week: lundi, mardi. Names of months: juillet, août.

(6) Members of religious sects, adherents of

political movements (and their derivative adjectives): les juifs, les musulmans, chrétien(ne),
calviniste, calvinisme, humaniste, protestant(e),
jansénisme, janséniste, romantisme, romantique,
socialisme, socialiste.

In plays the dramatis personae at the head of
scenes are put in large capitals, and those not named
in even small capitals:

SCÈNE V

TRIBOULET, BLANCHE, HOMMES,
FEMMES DU PEUPLE

In the dialogues the names of the speakers are put in
even small capitals, and placed in the centre of the
line. The stage directions and the asides are put in
smaller type,[1] and are in the text; if verse, in parentheses over the words they refer to. If there are two
stage directions in one and the same line, it will be
advisable to split the line, thus:

(Revenu sur ses pas.)
Oublions-les! restons. —

(Il l'assied sur un banc.)
Sieds-toi sur cette pierre.

Directions not relating to any particular speaker
are set, if short, full right:

Celui que l'on croit mort n'est pas mort. — Le
voici!   (Étonnement général.)

Division of words

Words should be divided according to spoken
syllables, as in what the French call *épellation* (i.e.
syllabication), and in only a few cases according to
etymology. A single consonant always goes with the
following vowel (amou-reux, cama-rade), groups
consisting of consonant + *r* or + *l* counting as
single consonants for this purpose (pa-trie, ca-price,

[1] Or in text italic.

li-vraison); other groups are divided thus: trans-porter, trans-poser, but divide transi-tion, transi-ger as shown. Doubled consonants may be divided: mil-lion, pil-lard, in-nocent. It is optional to divide ob-scurité or obs-curité, according to convenience. Vowels are divided only in compound words: e.g. extra-ordinaire; not Mo-abite, mo-yen.

In compound and hyphenated words an apostrophe is divided from a consonant following, thus: prud'-homme.

Divide sei-gneur, indi-gnité (gn, a single sound, pronounced roughly like *ni* in 'mania'), i.e. take gn over.

The following divisions should be avoided: Ma-ximilien, soi-xante, Me-xique; é-légant. In a narrow measure a syllable of two letters may stand at the end of a line: ce-pendant, in-décis; but a syllable of two letters must not be taken over to the next line; therefore élégan-ce, adversi-té, are not permissible; but élégan-ces, mar-que, abri-cot, are tolerated.

Avoid terminating a paragraph with only the final syllable of a word in the last line.

Verbs taking the so-called euphonic *t* should always be divided before the latter, thus: Viendra-|t-il?

Never divide abbreviated words.

Mute syllables, provided they are of more than two letters, may be turned over to the next line, thus: ils don-nent, les hom-mes.

Grave and acute accents

Certain words such as collège, avènement, etc., once often spelt with an acute accent, are now regularly spelt with a grave accent. The following is a list of the most common:

allège	avènement	le Corrège
l'Ariège	barège	cortège
arpège	collège	florilège

grège	la Norvège	sacrilègement
lège	*or* Norwège	siège
liège, Liège[1]	piège	solfège
manège	privilège	sortilège
mège	sacrilège	sphège

Hyphens

Place-names containing an article or the prepositions *en*, *de*, should have a hyphen between the component parts, thus: Saint-Germain-des-Prés, Saint-Valéry-en-Caux; but no hyphen between the introductory *le* or *la* and the noun in such names as la Ferté-Milon, la Ferté-sous-Jouarre.

Names of places, public buildings, or streets, to which one or more distinguishing words are added, usually take hyphens: Saint-Étienne-du-Mont, Vitry-le-François, rue du Faubourg-Montmartre, le Pont-Neuf, le Palais-Royal, but Hôtel des Monnaies. Distinguish Saint-Martin de Tours (the church of St. Martin situated at Tours) and Saint-Martin-de-Laigle (where the name of the church is the same as that of the parish in which it is, or was, situated). Composite place-names are hyphenated, e.g. Saint-Denis-de-la-Réunion.

Hyphens are used to connect cardinal and ordinal numbers in words under 100: e.g. vingt-quatre; trois cent quatre-vingt-dix; but when *et* joins two cardinal numbers no hyphen is used, e.g. vingt et un; cinquante et un. But print ordinal numbers with hyphens, as vingt-et-unième.

Italic and roman type

In algebraical formulae the capital letters are always put in roman and the small letters in italic. If, however, the text is in italic, the small letters are put in roman.

[1] Belgian official spelling since 1946, replacing traditional Liége.

Titles of works, plays, and journals, names of ships, of statues, and titles of tables mentioned in the text, are put in italic; thus: La pièce *La Chatte blanche*; J'ai vu *Les Rois en exil*; On lit dans *Le Figaro*; le journal *Le Temps*; le transport *Bien-Hoa*.

Foreign words and short quotations[1] are, as in English, italicized: *Cave canem!* lisait-on …

Superior letters in words italicized should be in italic, thus: *Histoire de Napoléon Ier*.

Metal-rules

These serve in French to denote conversational matter, and take a thick space (or more, if necessary) after them. In fact, metal-rules, as in German, always have a space before and after, and are never put close to a word as with the English dash. They are likewise never put after colons.

They are also used (with thin spaces) to give more force to a point: Il avait un cœur d'or, — mais une tête folle; et vraiment, — je puis le dire, — il était d'un caractère très agréable.

They are likewise used, as in English, for intercalations: Cette femme — étrangère sans doute — était très âgée.

Numerals

When cardinal numbers are expressed in roman lower-case letters, the final unit should be expressed by a j, not an i, thus: ij, iij, vj, viij.

Numbers are put in words if only occasionally occurring in the text. If used statistically, figures are used.

Degrees of temperature are given thus: 15°, 15; degrees of latitude and longitude, as in English, 15° 15′.

Age must be given in words, e.g. huit ans, and also times of day, if expressed in hours and fractions of

---

[1] That is, words foreign to French.

hours, e.g. six heures, trois heures et quart. But time expressed in minutes, e.g. 6 h. 15 m. or 6 h. 00 m., should be set in figures.

Dates, figures, etc., are put in words in legal documents: l'an mil neuf cent quatre (the year one thousand nine hundred and four).

In figures middle spaces are used to divide thousands, thus: 20 250 fr. 25 or 20 250^{fr},25. But dates, and numbers in general, are always put without a space: l'année 1466; page 1250; Code civil, art. 2000.

One should not put 'de 5 à 6 000 hommes', but 'de 5 000 à 6 000 hommes'.

Fractions with a horizontal stroke are preferred in mathematical and scientific works; but in ordinary works the diagonal stroke can be used, thus: 1/2, 2/3 (½, ⅔).

In logarithm tables the fractional part of a logarithm is printed with spaces, thus: Log. 2670 = 3, 426 5113; and also: Log. 2670 = 3, 4 265 113.

Punctuation

In general, French punctuation is rhetorical, not logical, and tends to be lighter than English: e.g. commas are often used where English would have colons or semicolons, and the comma is omitted before 'et' in enumerations. However, the comma is more freely used than in English to set off an adverbial complement at the beginning of a sentence: Sur la rivière, on voyait un bateau.

Quotation marks

In books (including lectures) completely in French use special quotation marks « » (called guillemets). A guillemet is repeated at the head of every subsequent paragraph belonging to the quotation.

In conversational matter guillemets are sometimes put at the beginning and end of the remarks, and the individual utterances are denoted by a metal-rule (spaced). But it is more common to dispense with guillemets altogether, and to denote the speakers by a metal-rule only. This is an important variation from the English method.

If the » comes after 'points de suspension' (see pp. 95–6), a thin space is put before it:

> La cour a décrété qu' « attendu l'urgence... »

If, in dialogue, a passage is quoted, the « is put before the metal-rule:

> « — Demain, à minuit, nous sortirons enfin! »

In tables and workings the » is used to denote an absent quantity:

$$125 \;.\; 15 \qquad\qquad 130 \qquad »$$
$$10 \qquad » \qquad\qquad 15 \;.\; 25$$

When a sentence contains a quotation, the point at the end of the latter is put before the », and the point belonging to the sentence after:

> « Prenez garde au chien! », lisait-on à l'entrée des maisons romaines.

If the matter quoted ends with a full stop, and a comma follows in the sentence, the full stop is suppressed:

> « C'est par le sang et par le fer que les États grandissent », a dit Bismarck.

Also, if the point at the end of the quotation is a full stop, and the sentence ends with a question or exclamation mark, the full stop is suppressed:

> A-t-il dit: « Je reviendrai » ?

When quotation and sentence end with the same point, or when the sentence ends with a full stop, only the quotation is pointed:

Quel bonheur d'entendre: « Je vous aime! »
A-t-il dit: « Qui est ici? »
Il a dit: « Je viendrai. »

But if the punctuation at the end of a quotation differs from that of the sentence, both points are put:

A-t-il dit: « Quel grand malheur ! » ?

Put before opening and after closing guillemets the space used between words.

In a quotation within a quotation, the « must stand at the commencement of each line of the enclosed quotation:

On lit dans *Le Radical:* « Une malheureuse erreur a été commise par un de nos artistes du boulevard. Ayant à dire: « Mademoiselle, je ne veux qu'un mot de vous! », il a fait entendre ces paroles: « Mademoiselle, je ne veux « qu'un mou de veau! »

When every line begins with a guillemet, put a thin space after the « commencing each line.

Only one » is put at the end of two quotations ending simultaneously.

Reference figures

References to notes are generally rendered thus: (1), or thus: [1]. Sometimes an asterisk between parentheses (*) or standing alone *, or italic superior letter [a], is used. Superior figures not enclosed in parentheses are the best from the English point of view.

The figure in the note itself is put either 1. or (1) or [1]. In many works the reference figure is put [1], and the note figure 1.

Spacing

No spaces are to be put before the 'points de suspension', i.e. three points close together, cast in one piece, denoting an interruption (...). Colons, section-marks, daggers, and double daggers take a thin space before or after them. Asterisks and superior figures, not enclosed in parentheses, referring to notes, usually take a thin space before them. Points of suspension are always followed by a space. For guillemets see pp. 93–4.

A space is put after an apostrophe following a word of two or more syllables (as a Frenchman reckons syllables, e.g. bonne is a word of two syllables):

> Bonn' petite... Aimabl' enfant!...

Spaces are put in such a case as 10 h. 15 m. 10 s. (10 hours 15 min. 10 sec.), also printed 10^h 15^m 10^s.

GERMAN

A useful reference-book for German spelling and style of printing is Duden, *Rechtschreibung der deutschen Sprache und der Fremdwörter*, 15. Auflage, Mannheim, 1961, Bibliographisches Institut AG.

ROMAN (*Antiqua*) type is now normally used in German-speaking countries; but German types (*Fraktur* and *Schwabacher*) are still used to a limited extent in Germany both for bookwork and for jobbing.

German sorts in roman type. In addition to the roman alphabet used in England, the following extra sorts are required for the German language: the vowels with the mark for an *Umlaut* Ä, Ö, Ü, ä, ö, ü, and the *Eszett* ß.[1] The combinations ch, ck, and tz, sometimes provided by German typefounders with roman types, need not be used: all that is necessary is to remember that when these

---

[1] There are no corresponding capital and small capital letters: SS is used.

letters occur together they must not be separated in
letter-spacing or when breaking words. The ligatures
ffi and ffl should NOT be used in setting German.
Use 2-piece f l in Auflage; 1-piece fl in Aufl.

Sorts in German type. The following are the
sorts normally provided in *Fraktur* types with their
roman equivalents:

𝔄 𝔄 𝔅 ℭ 𝔇 𝔈 𝔉 𝔊 ℌ   ℑ   𝔎 𝔏 𝔐 𝔑 𝔒 𝔒 𝔓 𝔔 𝔔
A Ä B C D E F G H I *or* J K L M N O Ö P Q R

𝔖 𝔗 𝔘 𝔘 𝔙 𝔚 𝔛 𝔜 𝔷
S T U Ü V W X Y Z

a ä b c d e f g h i j k l m n o ö p q r ſ s t u ü v w
a ä b c d e f g h i j k l m n o ö p q r ſ s t u ü v w

x y z   ch ck ff fi fl ll ſi ſſ ſt ß tz
x y z   ch ck ff fi fl ll ſi ſſ ſt ß tz

Abbreviations

The customary German abbreviations are followed
by full points, and thin spaces are put after full points
within them. Examples are: a. a. O. (am angeführten
Ort), Dr. (Doktor), Frl. (Fräulein), usw. (und so
weiter).

The abbreviations for metric measures and weights
are not followed by full points: mm, cm, m, qm or m^2,
cbm or m^3; l, hl; g, kg, dz, t (see list in French section, pp. 83–4).

A number of abbreviations of recent origin are set
in capital letters and are not followed by full points:
e.g. AG (Aktiengesellschaft), DDR (Deutsche
Demokratische Republik), HO (Handelsorganisa-
tion).[1]

In German texts print figures in full: 27–28,
331–335.

[1] But note: GmbH. (Gesellschaft mit beschränkter
Haftung), Jg. (Jahrgang), Jgg. (Jahrgänge), Jh. (Jahrhundert
or Jahrhunderte), WO. (Wechselordnung).

Accented letters

It is permissible to use roman accented letters and letters with cedilla with German type when setting foreign words (e.g. Café, Alençon).

Apostrophe

The apostrophe is used to mark the elision of *e* to render colloquial usage: e.g. Wie geht's, ich komm'; but not if the elision has been accepted in literary language: e.g. unsre, die andren. When the apostrophe occurs at the beginning of a sentence, the following letter does not therefore become a capital: 's brennt (*not* 'S brennt).

It is also used to mark the suppression of the possessive *s* (for reasons of euphony) after names ending in s, ß, x, z: Voß' Luise, Demosthenes' *Reden*, Aristoteles' *Werke*, Horaz' *Oden*.

Division of words

Avoid dividing words of one syllable or turning over fewer than three letters to the next line. Simple (as opposed to compound) words should be divided by syllables, either between consonants: e.g. Fin-ger, fal-len, An-ker, Red-ner, war-ten; or after a vowel followed by a single consonant: e.g. lo-ben, tra-gen, Va-ter. When a division has to be made between three or more consonants, the last should be turned over: e.g. Vermitt-ler, Abwechs-lung, Derff-linger, kämp-fen, kämpf-ten. But certain combinations of consonants must not be separated: these are ch, ph, sch, ß, th (representing single sounds), and st. Correct examples are: spre-chen, wa-schen, So-phie, ka-tholisch, La-sten, Fen-ster, wech-seln, Wechs-ler. For historical reasons, if a word is broken at the combination ck, it is represented as though spelt with kk: thus Zucker, but Zuk-ker; Glocken, but Glok-ken.

For this purpose words with suffixes are considered as simple words and divided in accordance with the rules given above: Bäcke-rei, le-bend, Liefe-rung.

Compound words may be broken into their etymological constituents in accordance with the rules for simple words: e.g. Bürger-meister, Haus-frau, Armband-uhr; and prefixes may be separated from the root-word: e.g. be-klagen, emp-fehlen, er-obern, aus-trinken, ab-wechseln, zer-splittern. Germans break foreign words in the same way as their own, distinguishing between simple and compound words.

Three identical letters are not written before a vowel, though they sometimes occur before a consonant: e.g. stickstofffrei, *but* Brennessel, Schiffahrt; but when a word is broken, the turned-over element recovers its initial consonant: Brenn-nessel, Schiff-fahrt. The divisions Mit-tag, den-noch are exceptions.

Double letters

The ligatures that occur only in German types, ch, ck, ſch, ſt, ll, ſi, ſſ, ß, tz, and the f-ligatures fi, fl, ff (which occur in roman also) and ft, must not be used so as to join the etymologically distinct elements in German words, for example the prefix or suffix with the root-word or the parts of a compound word; e.g. schlaflos, *not* schlaflos; verwerflich, *not* verwerflich; auffahren, *not* auffahren; achtzig, *not* achtzig; vielleicht, *not* vielleicht; Dekorationstuch, *not* Dekorationstuch. When in doubt, use single letters.

Hyphens

Compound words are written both with and without hyphens in German, as in English; a noun

after a hyphen commences with an initial capital:
Mozart-Konzertabend, Schiller-Museum, Kaiser
Wilhelm-Institut, Kaiser-Wilhelm-Kanal. The
ruling of Duden should be followed. When part
of a compound word is omitted to save repetition,
the hyphen is used to mark the suppression: e.g.
Feld- und Gartenfrüchte, ein- und ausatmen. In
this case the hyphen is followed by the space of the
line (or preceded by it, as in Jugendlust und -leid).
The hyphen is used to avoid the double repetition
of a vowel, e.g. Kaffee-Ersatz, but not to avoid the
similar repetition of a consonant, e.g. stickstofffrei.

Initial capitals

All nouns in German are written with initial capital
letters. Adjectives, numerals, and the infinitives of
verbs, if used as nouns, are also given initial capitals:
Gutes und Böses; die Drei; Sagen und Tun ist
zweierlei. The pronouns Sie and Ihr have capitals
when they mean 'you' and 'your'. Adjectives have
initial capitals when forming part of a geographical
name, e.g. Kap der Guten Hoffnung, Schwarzes
Meer, or the names of historic events or eras, e.g. die
Französische Revolution (of 1789), der Dreißig-
jährige Krieg, have initial capitals. German adjectives derived from personal names are given initial
capitals when they are used to denote only association with the person from whose name they derive,
e.g. die Grimmschen Märchen (*Grimm's Fairy
Tales*), die Lutherische Bibelübersetzung (Luther's
translation of the Bible); but when they are
used in a more general sense, the initial capital is
dropped, e.g. die lutherische Kirche (the Lutheran
Church), ein napoleonischer Unternehmungsgeist
(a Napoleonic spirit of enterprise). Adjectives
denoting nationality have no initial capitals: das
deutsche Vaterland; die italienische Küste. The
word 'von' of personal names is written with a

lower-case initial, but with a capital at the beginning
of a sentence unless it is abbreviated to v., when
a lower-case initial is used to avoid confusion with
the initial of a Christian name.

Letter-spacing for emphasis

Letter-spacing is the means adopted for emphasiz-
ing words in *Fraktur* type (as italic is used for
emphasis in English practice). When setting roman,
German printers use letter-spacing or italic or small
capitals for emphasis. In letter-spaced matter spaces
are put before the punctuation marks excepting the
full point. The combinations ch (ch), ck (ck), tz (tz) are
to be regarded as single letters, and must not be
spaced apart.

Numerals

A number of more than four figures should be
separated in thousands by thin spaces: e.g. 6 580 340.
The comma in German practice marks the decimal
point (it is used in writing amounts of money in
decimal coinage: e.g. 15,00 DM, or 0,75 DM). A
full point after a numeral shows that it represents
an ordinal number: e.g. 14. Auflage (14th edition);
Friedrich II. war König; Mittwoch, 18. Juli 1956.
The full point also marks the separation of hours
from minutes: e.g. 14.30 Uhr.

Punctuation

German practice differs from English in a few re-
spects. Subordinate clauses beginning with daß and
relative clauses (beginning, e.g., with der, die, das,
welche, womit, wodurch) are preceded by a comma:
e.g. Er sagte, daß... (he said that, etc.); Ich höre,
daß... Exception: if daß is preceded by a conjunction, the comma is set before the conjunction:
e.g. Ich höre, daß du nichts erspart hast, sondern
daß du sogar noch die Ersparnisse deiner Frau

vergeudest. Er beeilte sich, so daß er den Zug noch erreichte.

Square brackets are used for parentheses within parentheses. Em rules (and longer rules) are preceded and followed by spaces.

Quotation marks

German quotation marks take the form of two commas at the beginning of the quotation, and two turned commas at the end. Quotations within quotations are marked by a single comma at the beginning and a turned comma at the end. The quotation marks are not separated by spaces from the quotation. Punctuation following a quotation is put after the closing quotation mark. French guillemets, but pointing inwards (» «), are now preferred by some German printers to the traditional German quotation marks.

Use of ſ and ß

The long ſ is used in setting *Fraktur* type at the beginnings of words, and within them except at the ends of syllables. The short final -s is put at the ends of syllables and words (see Duden). The ß in roman type is equivalent to the ß in *Fraktur* types, but it must not be used for every -ss-, as, for example, in such words as dasselbe, Eisscholle, where the first s ends a syllable or etymologically distinct part of a word or compound. By way of exception, in *Fraktur* type the long ſ is used at the ends of syllables before p: e.g. Weſpe, Knoſpe. The ß or ß is not divided when words are broken at the ends of lines: e.g. ɦei=ßen, genie-ßen.

GREEK

THE Greek alphabet consists of twenty-four letters —seventeen consonants and seven vowels. The vowels are: α, ε, η, ι, ο, υ, ω.

The following is the order of the letters:

A	α	alpha		*N*	ν	nu
B	β	beta		*Ξ*	ξ	xi
Γ	γ	gamma		*O*	o	omicron
Δ	δ	delta		*Π*	π	pi
E	ε	epsilon		*P*	ρ	rho
Z	ζ	zeta		*Σ*	σ	(ς final) or c sigma
H	η	eta		*T*	τ	tau
Θ	θ	theta		*Υ*	υ	upsilon
I	ι	iota		*Φ*	φ	phi
K	κ	kappa		*X*	χ	chi
Λ	λ	lambda		*Ψ*	ψ	psi
M	μ	mu		*Ω*	ω	omega

ϙ (koppa) and ϡ (sampi) are obsolete letters used only as signs for 90 and 900 respectively, see *Cardinal numbers* below.

Aspirates and accents

'	Lenis (smooth)	'	Asper grave
'	Asper (rough)	^	Circumflex
'	Acute	'	Circumflex lenis
`	Grave	'	Circumflex asper
'	Lenis acute	¨	Diaeresis
'	Lenis grave	'	Diaeresis acute
'	Asper acute	'	Diaeresis grave

The acute (') is only used upon one of the last three syllables of a word.

The grave (`) can only be used upon the last syllable of a word.

The circumflex (^) occurs upon either the last syllable of a word, or the last but one.

The Greek vowels allow of two breathings: the asper or rough ('), which the Greeks use instead of the letter *h*; and the lenis or smooth ('), which denotes the absence of the *h*.

All vowels beginning a word have a breathing over them; but upsilon (υ) allows of no other than the asper. In diphthongs (αι, ει, οι, υι, αυ, ευ, ηυ, ου, ωυ) the breathing stands over the second vowel (thus: υἱ, οὐ) as do accents.

The initial letter ρ takes the asper

Double ρρ was formerly printed ῤῥ ('horns'), but should now always be ρρ.

The lenis (᾿) is used for eliding the vowels α, ε, ι, ο, and sometimes the diphthongs αι and οι, when they stand at the end of a word or syllable, followed by another vowel beginning a word or syllable. Elision takes place in all the prepositions, except περι and προ. Sometimes it unites two words.

When there is fusion of two syllables, the breathing is on the fused vowel or diphthong, the aspirate becoming 'smooth' when the first consonant takes the 'rough' breathing of the second word; e.g. τὸ ἐπί = τοὐπί; τὸ ἱμάτιον = θοἰμάτιον; καὶ ἡ = χἠ; πρό + ἔχω = προὔχω.

The diaeresis (¨) is used to separate two vowels from each other, and to prevent their being taken for a diphthong.

Note the following rules: no word can have an *accent* except over one of the last three syllables; the *grave* (᾿) over the last syllable of a word; and the *asper grave* (῝) and *lenis grave* (῎) over a few monosyllables.

The majority of words in the Greek language have an *accent*, and rarely have more than one; when this occurs, it is an *acute* thrown back upon the last syllable from an enclitic, which is not accented except when it is followed by another enclitic. No word can have an *acute* accent over the last syllable except in this case, or before a comma, full point, colon, or interrogation, when the *grave* is changed to an *acute*.

When a Greek word accented grave on its last syllable appears in an English context and is followed by English words, its grave accent is changed to acute.

Cardinal numbers

1	a'	18	$\iota\eta'$	500	ϕ'
2	β'	19	$\iota\theta'$	600	χ'
3	γ'	20	κ'	700	ψ'
4	δ'	21	$\kappa a'$	800	ω'
5	ϵ'	22	$\kappa\beta'$	900	$\lambdaarrow'$
6	s'	23	$\kappa\gamma'$	1,000	$,a$
7	ζ'	30	λ'	2,000	$,\beta$
8	η'	40	μ'	3,000	$,\gamma$
9	θ'	50	ν'	4,000	$,\delta$
10	ι'	60	ξ'	5,000	$,\epsilon$
11	$\iota a'$	70	o'	6,000	$,s$
12	$\iota\beta'$	80	π'	7,000	$,\zeta$
13	$\iota\gamma'$	90	$\digamma'$	8,000	$,\eta$
14	$\iota\delta'$	100	ρ'	9,000	$,\theta$
15	$\iota\epsilon'$	200	σ'	10,000	$,\iota$
16	$\iota s'$	300	τ'	20,000	$,\kappa$
17	$\iota\zeta'$	400	υ'	100,000	$,\rho$

Division of Greek and Latin words

Usually a vowel can be divided from another:

$$\text{be-atus, } \lambda\acute{\upsilon}\text{-}\omega\nu$$

but some combinations form one sound, a diphthong, one syllable only:

$$ae, \ au, \ eu, \ oe, \ a\iota, \ a\upsilon, \ \epsilon\iota, \ \epsilon\upsilon, \ \eta\upsilon, \ o\iota, \ o\upsilon, \ \upsilon\iota$$

and these must not be divided.

Difficulties arise from consonants. As in English, a single consonant is normally taken over; but also (unlike English) any combination of consonants which can begin a word in Greek or Latin should be taken over, not split. Most are easily recognizable, as able to begin words in English also, e.g. br-, cl-, sm-, tr-; but among the less expected are:

ct- and $\kappa\tau$- fa-ctus, $\dot{\epsilon}\lambda\iota$-$\kappa\tau\acute{o}s$
gn-, $\gamma\nu$- (gnat, gnaw) di-gnus, $\gamma\iota$-$\gamma\nu\acute{\omega}$-$\sigma\kappa\omega$
mn-, $\mu\nu$- (mnemonic) da-mnum, $\mu\iota$-$\mu\nu\acute{\eta}$-$\sigma\kappa\omega$

pn-, πν- (pneumonia) hy-pnotice, κα-πνός
ps-, (ψ-) (psychology) la-psus, (ἀνε-ψιός)
pt-, ππ- (ptomaine, sum-ptus, βα-πτί-ζω
  Ptolemy)
x-, ξ- (xylophone) pro-xi-mus, Ἀλέ-ξαν-
                      δρος

Particularly watch s: cre-sco, γι-γνώ-σκω
                si-ni-stra, ἀπο-στρέ-φω

and in Greek -σβ, -σγ, -σθ, -σκ, -στ, -σχ, which must
not be divided, except as below. In fact, usually take
s and σ over except for ss, σσ, which must neither
begin nor end a line.

Any doubled consonants may be divided; also,
apart from the above exception for m (μ), the letters
l, m, n, and r (Greek λ, μ, ν, and ρ) may be divided
from a following consonant.

In Greek γ may be divided from a following κ
or χ.

The above rules are subject to the overriding
rule that compound words are divided into their
parts. This rule may and does cut across the above
rules. It would help the compositor to be alert to
the following prefixes ending in consonants:

ab, ad, ex, ob, sub, εἰσ, ἐν, ἐξ, ἐσ, ξυν, προσ, συν.

Usually a division after these, even before a vowel,
will be correct.

In Greek ἀντι-, ἀπο-, ἐπι-, κατα-, μετα-, παρα-,
ὑπο- have their full form before a word-part beginning with a consonant: then divide as usual:

ἀπο-κνίζω, κατα-λύω.

But before a word-part beginning with a vowel (or
aspirated vowel) they become ἀντ- (ἀνθ-), ἀπ- (ἀφ-),
ἐπ- (ἐφ-), κατ- (καθ-), μετ- (μεθ-), παρ-, ὑπ- (ὑφ-),
and then it will be right to divide after the consonant:

ἀπ-αίρω, καθ-ήκω.

There are some other cases, chiefly compound words, where a more detailed knowledge of the language must decide.[1] The instances where the foregoing rules do not suffice will be few and can be left to specialist readers to adjust.

So, too, may those instances where the vowel of a preposition is cut off before the identical vowel. For example:

ὀκνῶ is a simple word: therefore ἀπ-οκνῶ is correct.

ἅπτομαι is a simple word: therefore παρ-άπτομαι is correct.

Punctuation

In Greek the comma, the full point, and the exclamation (in modern Greek) are the same as in English; but the question mark (;) is the English semicolon, and the colon is an inverted full point (·).

Use double quotes generally in Greek.

Spacing

In Greek and Latin, when a vowel is omitted at the end of a word (denoted by a lenis), put the ordinary spacing of the line before the word which immediately follows.

In Greek emphasized words should be 1-pt. spaced.

ITALIAN

Division of words

THE following compound consonants are not to be divided: bl, br; ch, cl, cr; dr; fl, fr; gh, gl, gn, gr; pl, pr; sb, sc, sd, sf, sg, sl, sm, sn, sp, sq, sr, st, sv; tl, tr; vr; sbr; sch; scr; sdr; sfr; sgh; sgr; spl; spr; str.

[1] e.g. hac-tenus, non-iam, red-ibo, sol-ueret, Ἀραβ-άρχης, δήμ-αρχος, Διοσ-κόρω, ὥσπερ-ανεί are correct divisions.

Generally in Italian words there are as many syllables as there are vowels. Words are divided into syllables, so that you have consonant plus vowel, or vowel standing alone; e.g. a-mo-re, pre-ci-pi-ta-re.

When a syllable has a diphthong or triphthong instead of a single vowel, the syllable always ends with the latter, e.g. ce-reo; neu-tro; fie-ro; chiu-so; pa-iuo-lo, fi-gliuo-lo. In these cases there are more vowels than syllables. In words ending with *ii*, if these two vowels form a diphthong they belong to the same syllable: pre-lu-dii; if not, the second *i* makes a syllable by itself: uaì-i; restì-i; pì-i.

When the vowel is followed by a doubled consonant, the first of these goes with the vowel, and the second is joined to the next syllable; i.e. the division comes between the two letters: lab-bro, mag-gio, som-ma, raz-zo. So also ac-qua, nac-que, noc-que, piac-que—these are really doubled consonants.

Groups of two or three consonants at the beginning of a word make a syllable with the vowel or diphthong: pro-va, gla-ciale, stra-zio, schio-dare. In the middle of a word, if the first consonant of a group is a liquid (i.e. either *l*, *m*, *n*, or *r*) it makes a syllable with the preceding vowel, and the other consonant, or combination of consonants, goes with the succeeding vowel: al-tero, ar-tigiano, tem-pra, stan-za.

In words which have the prefixes *as-*, *es-*, *dis-*, *tras-*, the words are divided so as to separate the entire prefix: as-trarre, es-posto, dis-fatta, tras-porto. If assimilation has taken place, we have, according to the foregoing rules, ef-fluvio, dif-ficile, dif-fuso.

Spacing

In Italian put the ordinary spacing of the line after an apostrophe following a vowel (and in this case when necessary the apostrophe may end a line); but there should be no space after an apostrophe following a consonant (in this case the apostrophe may not end a line): e.g. *a' miei, de' malevoli, i' fui, ne' righi, po' duro*; but *dall'aver, l'onda, s'allontana, senz'altro*. (Note that where an apostrophe replaces a vowel at the beginning of a word a space always precedes it, e.g. *e 'l, su 'l, te 'l, che 'l*.)

ORIENTAL LANGUAGES IN ROMAN TYPE

THE principal Oriental languages have alphabets of their own.

Often words or sentences in these languages have to be set up in roman type. But there is as yet no uniform fixed system of spelling words from any of these languages when set in roman. Therefore the system used in the copy should generally be followed as far as possible.

In Arabic (as in Aramaic, Hebrew, Persian, etc.) there are two letters which do not occur in the roman alphabet. These are *'ain* and *hamza* and are to be represented by a Greek asper and a lenis respectively.

Examples: *'ain* (asper) *'ālim, mu'allim, ḍā'.*
hamza (lenis) *'amīr, mu'allim, ḍā'.*

In each case the sign is to be treated as a letter of the alphabet and part of the word and must not be confused with a quotation mark. Note that an apostrophe, denoting elision, usually appears before *l* followed by a hyphen, e.g. *'Abdu 'l-Malik*. (N.B. The turned comma is not to be used for *'ain* unless specially ordered.)

In printing Arabic, etc., long vowels are to be represented by a stroke, not a circumflex, unless otherwise ordered: tawārī<u>kh</u>, not tawârîkh; ma'lūm, not ma'lûm.

In printing Ancient Egyptian words in roman type use the special sign ⟨ instead of the Greek asper ⟨, and strokes instead of circumflexes, e.g. Rē⟨, not Rê⟨.

RUSSIAN

THESE notes relate specifically to questions of orthography, punctuation, and typography which may arise when editing or setting matter in Russian.[1] *They are in principle restricted to points where English and Russian practice diverge.*

It should be stressed that many points cannot be fully covered by formal rules: a knowledge of Russian word-formation and syntax is often essential if correct decisions are to be reached in individual cases.

Russian is one of the six Slavonic languages that are written in Cyrillic script—the others being (in the U.S.S.R.) Belorussian (or White Russian) and Ukrainian, and (outside the U.S.S.R.) Bulgarian, Macedonian, and Serbian. The additional sorts called for by the five non-Russian languages are omitted from the table of the Cyrillic alphabet which follows, but details of them are given in the text below it. Bracketed letters were abolished (the ъ is, however, retained medially) when the New Orthography was introduced in Russia in 1918. They are still occasionally found in work published outside the U.S.S.R.

Additional sorts (including those eliminated in

[1] For fuller information about Russian orthography and punctuation see K. I. Bȳlinskiĭ and N. N. Nikol'skiĭ, *Spravochnik po orfografii i punktuatsii dlya rabotnikov pechati*, 4th ed. (Moscow, 1970) and *Pravila russkoĭ orfografii i punktuatsii*, 2nd ed. (Moscow, 1962).

1918) are used when setting Old Russian texts; Old Church Slavonic also calls for additional sorts, and is usually set in a face which bears the same relation to modern Russian types as black letter does to normal roman faces.

The table includes 'upright' (*pryamoĭ*) and 'cursive' (*kursiv*) forms and also a transliteration in accordance with the 'British System' as given in British Standard 2979:1958. For further information about transliteration see *Transliteration*.

А	а	*A*	*a*	a	С	с	*C*	*c*	s
Б	б	*Б*	*б*	b	Т	т	*T*	*m*	t
В	в	*B*	*в*	v	ТС	тс	*TC*	*mc*	t's
Г	г	*Г*	*г*	g	У	у	*У*	*y*	u
Д	д	*Д*	*д*	d	Ф	ф	*Ф*	*ф*	f
Е	е	*Е*	*е*	e	Х	х	*X*	*x*	kh
Ё	ё	*Ё*	*ё*	ë	Ц	ц	*Ц*	*ц*	ts
Ж	ж	*Ж*	*ж*	zh	Ч	ч	*Ч*	*ч*	ch
З	з	*З*	*з*	z	Ш	ш	*Ш*	*ш*	sh
И	и	*И*	*u*	i	Щ	щ	*Щ*	*щ*	shch
[I	i	*I*	*i*	ї]	[Ъ	ъ	*Ъ*	*ъ*	"]
Й	й	*Й*	*ŭ*	ĭ	Ы	ы	*Ы*	*ы*	ȳ
К	к	*К*	*к*	k	Ь	ь	*Ь*	*ь*	'
Л	л	*Л*	*л*	l	[Ѣ	ѣ	*Ѣ*	*ѣ*	ê]
М	м	*M*	*м*	m	Э	э	*Э*	*э*	é
Н	н	*Н*	*н*	n	Ю	ю	*Ю*	*ю*	yu
О	о	*O*	*o*	o	Я	я	*Я*	*я*	ya
П	п	*П*	*п*	p	[Ѳ	ѳ	*Ѳ*	*ѳ*	f]
Р	р	*P*	*p*	r	[V	ѵ		*ѵ*	ў]

Note that the substitution of the apostrophe for the hard sign (ъ), occasionally found in Russian texts, is incorrect.

The extra sorts called for by the other Cyrillic-using languages are: Belorussian ў (= *w*); Macedonian ѓ (= *đ*), ѕ (= *dz*), ј (= *j*), ќ (= *ć*), љ (= *lj*), њ (= *nj*), and џ (= *dž*); Serbian Ђ, ђ (= *đ*), ј (= *j*), љ (= *lj*), њ (= *nj*), Ћ, ћ (= *ć*), and џ (= *dž*); and

Ukrainian є (= *ye*), and ї (= *yi*) (ґ = *g* is now obsolete).

In some Macedonian and Serbian founts cursive г, п, and т are in the form of superior-barred cursive *ī*, *ū*, and *ū* respectively.

Abbreviations

Modern Russian non-literary texts abound in abbreviations. Details of these are available in D. I. Alekseev's dictionary—*Slovar' sokrashchenii russkogo yazȳka* (Moscow, 1963).

Abbreviations of compound terms formed from their initial letters are set in lower case, letter-spaced (except when hyphenated), and pointed, e.g. и т. д., и пр., *but* с.-д. Abbreviations by contraction, e.g. д-р, are unpointed.

Abbreviations consisting of capital initial letters, e.g. СССР, are set close without medial or final points. When declined, such abbreviations add flexional endings in closed-up lower case, e.g. ГОСТа.

Abbreviations for metric and other units used in scientific measurement are usually set in cursive and are not followed by a full point; abbreviated qualifying adjectives have the full point, however, e.g. 5 *кв. км*, etc.

Commonly used abbreviations which are pronounced syllabically and declined, e.g. вуз, are not followed by a full point.

Bibliographical lists[1]

The author's name should be letter-spaced and followed by his initials. Titles of books and articles

[1] A detailed account of the Russian method of describing titles in bibliographical lists is given in N. A. Nikiforovskaya's *Pravila bibliograficheskogo opisaniya proizvedenii pechati* (Leningrad, 1964).

(in upright) are *not* given within guillemets; titles of periodicals and newspapers are:

Тимирязев К. А. Земледелие и физиология растений. М.-Л., «Книга», 1965. 215 с.

Петрович Г. В. Через ближний космос во вселенную. — «Авиация и космонавтика», 1962, № 6, с. 8–12.

Transliterated matter should follow English practice.

Capital and lower case

Capital initial letters are in general less commonly used in Russian than in English.

Use lower-case initials for:

(*a*) Nouns and adjectives formed from personal names, e.g. толстовство, марксизм.

(*b*) Nationalities, names of nationals and of inhabitants of towns, e.g. таджик, Tadzhik; англичанин, Englishman; москвич, Moscovite.

(*c*) Adjectives formed from geographical names, except when they form part of a proper name or the name of an institution, e.g. европейские государства, European states; *but* Челябинский тракторный завод, Chelyabinsk Tractor Works.

(*d*) Non-proper-name elements in the titles of administrative areas of the U.S.S.R. other than Union or Autonomous Republics, e.g. Курганская область, Kurgan Region; *but* Туркменская Советская Социалистическая Республика, Turkmen Soviet Socialist Republic.

(*e*) Words (other than the first) in titles of international and non-Soviet organizations (other than of states) and societies, e.g. Американская федерация труда, American Federation of Labour.

(*f*) Words (other than the first) in titles of Soviet ministries, administrative organs, and Party and public organizations not of a 'unique' nature, e.g. Государственный комитет Совета Министров СССР по новой технике (note capitals for the 'unique' Совета Министров).

(*g*) Words (other than the first) in titles of institutions, except when the title begins with an adjective, e.g. Академия наук СССР, Academy of Sciences of the U.S.S.R.; *but* Государственный Исторический музей, State Historical Museum.

(*h*) Days of the week and names of the months, but note Первое мая and 1-е Мая for the May Day holiday (the capitalization in the latter form is due to the fact that the ordinal number does not count as the 'first word').

(*i*) Titles of literary works, newspapers, and journals, except for the first word and for proper names: роман «Отцы и дети»; опера «Иван Сусанин».

(*j*) Personal names used to indicate character: донжуан, a Don Juan; меценат, a Maecenas.

(*k*) Ranks, titles, etc.: св. Николай, St. Nicholas; князь Оболенский, Prince Obolenskiĭ; проф. Сидоров, Prof. Sidorov; полковник Иванов, Colonel Ivanov.

(*l*) Geographic terms forming part of the name of an area or place: остров Рудольфа, Rudolph Island; Северный полюс, the North Pole.

(*m*) The non-proper-name element in street and similar names: площадь Маяковского, Mayakovskiĭ Square.

(*n*) Names of wars, other than those with titles which refer directly to their character: франко-прусская война, Franco-Prussian War, *but* Великая Отечественная война, Great Patriotic War.

(*o*) Names (other than the first word) of historical events and battles: Кровавое воскресенье, Bloody Sunday; Полтавская битва, the Battle of Poltava.

(*p*) Names (other than the first word) of congresses, agreements, documents, prizes, etc.:

Вашингтонское соглашение, the Washington Agreement; Атлантийская хартия, the Atlantic Charter; Ленинская премия, Lenin Prize.

(*q*) The pronoun of the first person singular, я = I (except, of course, when used at the beginning of a sentence). Note that the personal and possessive pronouns of the second person plural (вы and ваш, etc.) take an initial capital when used of individuals in texts addressed to them, e.g. in letters.

The combination of capitals with small capitals is not found in Russian typography.

Dash

Dashes (em rules)[1] are much used in Russian texts, in particular:

(*a*) As a substitute for the copula in nominal statements: Волга — самая большая река в Европе, the Volga is the longest European river.

(*b*) To indicate omission of the verb, e.g. Один рабочий несёт астролябию, другой — треногу, one of the workmen carries the theodolite, the other the tripod.

(*c*) To indicate 'from ... to ...': 1946—1950, линия Москва—Горький (the Moscow–Gor'kiĭ line).

(*d*) Before, and to divide off, statements in dialogue set in paragraphs:

— Я вас люблю, — сказал князь.
— Простите...
— Что простить? — спросил князь Андрей.

Note that when dialogue is set continuously the direct-speech elements are divided off not only by dashes but also by guillemets: Десятник махнул рукой. «Мищенко вчера свой экскаватор утопил», — сказал он мрачно. — «Как? — вскипел Правдин. — Так это же сотни тысяч рублей!» — «Да, конечно!..» — согласился десятник...

[1] En rules are not used in Russian typography

Guillemets alone are used to distinguish occasional spoken words, e.g. Она громко закричала: «За мной!»

They are also used if the quoted words are from a letter or soliloquy, though the author's words are none the less divided off by dashes in such cases: «Боже мой, — подумал Мартин, — эта каналья разъезжает в пульмановских вагонах, а я голодаю!..» — Ярость охватила его.

Note in the above examples the use of the comma in addition to the dash to divide off the quoted from the author's words. Where the quoted words end with omission points or an exclamation or question mark, commas are not required. This rule applies whether or not guillemets are present.

Division of words

Russian syllables end in a vowel, and word-division is basically syllabic. However, there are many exceptions to this generalization, most of which are connected with Russian word-formation.

A consonant should not be separated from the prefix, root, or suffix of which it forms a part, e.g. род-|ной, под-|бежать, мещан-|ство are correct divisions.

Divide between double consonants, e.g. клас-| сы, except where this conflicts with the preceding ru e.

The letters ъ, ь, and й should never be separated from the letter preceding them, e.g. подъ-|езд.

Do not divide between initials; try to avoid dividing between initials and a surname.

Abbreviated titles, e.g. проф., ул. (before a street-name), should not be separated from the name to which they relate.

Letter abbreviations, e.g. РСФСР, ТУ-104, и т. д., may not be divided.

A single letter or two or more consonants without a vowel may not be either hyphenated at the end of a line or carried over: к-|руглый, ст-|рела, жидко-|сть are incorrect.

Hyphens

The hyphen is used:

(*a*) In nouns consisting of two noun elements, one of which reinforces or qualifies the sense of the other, and which are linked without an interpolated vowel: генерал-губернатор, Governor-General, *but* кровообращение, circulation of the blood.

(*b*) In compound place-names (and derived adjectives); consisting of (i) two nouns or a noun and an adjective, e.g. Каменец-Подольск, Нью-Йорк, *but* Чехословакия, Вышний Волочок (agreeing adjective); or (ii) two nouns joined by a preposition or conjunction, e.g. Рио-де-Жанейро; or (iii) which begin with a preposition, particle, or the word Сан, e.g. Ла-Плата, Сан-Франциско, *but* Ламанш, The Channel.

(*c*) In names incorporating the words сквер or стрит, e.g. Сохо-сквер.

(*d*) In compound points of the compass (nouns and adjectives).

(*e*) In compound adjectives (i) derived from nouns with complementary meanings, as, for example, журнально-газетный, periodical and newspaper; or (ii) indicating shades of colour: темно-коричневый, dark-brown.

Italic and letter-spacing

Italic (*kursiv*; cursive) and letter-spacing (*razryadka*) are used to distinguish or emphasize a word or words in the text. Of the two methods, letter-spacing is perhaps the more commonly employed for this purpose, though words cited in linguistic texts are always given in cursive. Guillemets are used to show that a word is being used in an un-familiar or special sense.

Titles of books and journals should be printed in upright type and not in cursive (see *Bibliographical lists* above).

Numerals, dates, reference figures, fractions

Numbers from 10,000 upwards are divided off into thousands by thin spaces, and not by commas, e.g. 26 453; below 10,000 they are set close, e.g. 9999.

The decimal comma is used in place of the decimal point, e.g. 0,36578.

Ordinal numbers are followed by a contracted adjectival termination except when they are used in dates: 5-й год *but* 7 ноября 1917 г.

Superior footnote-reference figures in the text precede punctuation marks and are followed by a thin space, e.g. ...ero[1] . In the footnote itself the reference figure or symbol is a superior and is followed by a space but no point.

The form of fraction with an oblique divider (solidus) is preferred, e.g. $^1/_5$ (except in mathe-matical work).

Inclusive dates are not abbreviated, e.g. 1946—1950. A financial or academic year which covers parts of two calendar years is expressed thus: 1946/47.

Plays

In dialogue the names of the speakers usually pre-cede the words spoken and are either letter-spaced or, less often, set in bold. They are also found centred. Stage directions, if set immediately after the name of the speaker or within the body, or at the end, of the spoken words, are set in cursive within parentheses:

Лопахин. Пришёл поезд, слава Богу. Который час?

Дуняша. Скоро два. (*Тушит свечу.*) Уже светло.

General stage directions are set centrally (or full left and with their last line centred) in upright but smaller type.

Punctuation

The chief points of difference between the Russian and the English punctuation systems relate to the use of the comma, omission points, and dashes. For the last see *Dash*; for guillemets see also *Dash*, *Italic and letter-spacing*, and *Quotation marks*; for punctuation of abbreviations see *Abbreviations*.

The comma is used more often than in English, and always:

(*a*) Before subordinate clauses introduced by interrogative-relative pronouns and adverbs, participles, and gerunds.

(*b*) To divide off co-ordinate clauses joined by conjunctions such as и, да, а, но, или.

(*c*) Between a principal clause and a subordinate clause introduced by a conjunction. Note that when the conjunction что forms the second element of a compound conjunction, the comma precedes the first part unless it is desired to stress the close causal or temporal connection between the two parts of the sentence:

Люди умирали, потому что была эпидемия.

People were dying, for there was an epidemic.

Люди умирали потому, что была эпидемия.

There was an epidemic, so people were dying.

In substantival and adjectival enumerations in which there is a single, final и, it is not preceded by a comma.

For the use of the comma in conjunction with the dash, see *Dash* (last paragraph).

The three dots indicating an interruption (omission points) are in one piece. They are always spaced at their open end (except when guillemets precede or follow), and set close at their engaged end, e.g. Это... я... умираю; ...уже; *but* «...мы должны отвергнуть». When omission points coincide with an exclamation or question mark, they form one piece with it and are reduced to two points: !.., ?..

Omission points are never immediately followed by a full point.

Where omission points (or an exclamation or question mark) precede quotation marks, the latter are never followed by a full point, e.g. «За мной!»

Quotation marks

Two forms of quotation mark are used in Russian: (i) opening double commas on the line followed by closing superior turned double commas (*lapochki*), and (ii) (double) guillemets (*ёlochki*). Of the two, guillemets are by far the more common form but in the remarks which follow the word will be taken to cover both forms of quotation mark.

Apart from their use to indicate direct speech and soliloquy (see *Dash* (*d*)), guillemets are used (*a*) to show that a word or words are being employed in a special sense, and (*b*) with titles of literary works, journals, and pictures, and with names of ships, factories, and organizations (except when the latter consist of initials or conventional abbreviations), e.g. роман «Война и мир», журнал «Новый мир», картина Репина «Не ждали», завод «Серп и молот», издательство «Книга», *but* Госиздат, ГЭС.

Quotation marks are not duplicated unless they are of differing design, e.g. Он ответил: «Я приехал вчера на пароходе «Казань» (note the final guillemet which covers both the end of the name of the ship and the end of the sentence); *but* Он ответил: „Я приехал вчера на пароходе «Казань»".

For the use of guillemets in bibliographical lists see *Bibliographical lists*; for punctuation after quotation marks see *Dash* and *Punctuation*.

Spacing

The dash (except between numerals and when linking extremities, when it is set close) is thin-spaced at either end; all other punctuation marks are set close.

For spacing of omission points see *Punctuation* (last three paragraphs).

Transliteration

The British Standard scheme given in the Table on p. 111 has much to commend it. It may be used with or without diacritics, though in the latter case it loses the advantage of reversibility. If desired, -*y* may be used to express final -ŭ, -uŭ, iŭ, and -ый in proper names, e.g. Tolstoy, Dostoevsky, Grozny. Another commonly used British system agrees with the British Standard scheme with the following exceptions: e = *ye* initially and after ъ, ь, or a vowel; ё = *yo* (*o* after ж, ч, ш or щ); й = *y*; final -ий, -ый = *y* in proper names or titles.

For philological work the International System (ISO/R9 = Table C in British Standard 2979: 1958) is recommended.

A comparative table covering seven transliteration systems is printed on p. 65 of R. Neiswender's *Guide to Russian Reference and Language Aids* (New York, 1962).

SPANISH

Accent

ACCENT in Spanish does not indicate vowel quality, nor musical pitch, but stress. This is indicated by the acute (´) accent. The only other diacritical marks used are the tilde on the *ñ*, which is a separate letter in the alphabet and follows *n* in indexes, etc., and the diaeresis on *ü*, which is used after *g* before *e* or *i* when *u* forms a diphthong with *e* or *i* and is not merely used to indicate hard *g* before *e* or *i*. (See under *Orthography*.)

There are two kinds of stress, the *normal* and the *abnormal*. The normal stress is never indicated by an accent; the abnormal stress is always indicated by the acute.

The normal stress occurs as follows:

(1) Words ending in a consonant, except *n* or *s*, have the stress on the last syllable; but proper names ending in *ez* and *iz* are usually stressed on the last but one. Examples: ciudad, reloj; carmen, intereses; but Cádiz, Páez, Vázquez, Velázquez.

(2) Words ending in a vowel or *n* or *s* have the stress on the last syllable but one. Where diphthongs occur in a stressed syllable the stress will fall on the strong vowel (*a, e, o*) if there is one, or on the second of two weak vowels (*i, u*). The stressed vowel is not marked, unless it occurs in an abnormally accented syllable. See below.

Abnormal stress. Words in which the stress falls otherwise than in accordance with the above rules must bear the printed accent, as trágico, amén, país, armonía, hebraísta, héroes (three syllables), piélago, tráiganoslas.

The termination *-ción*, equivalent to English *-tion*, always takes the acute on the *o* (though there is a tendency in modern newspapers to omit it, even in Spain). The plural form *-ciones* requires no accent.

The words *a* ('to'), *e* ('and'), *o*, *u* ('or') are now printed without accents.

The words ¿cuál?, ¿cómo?, ¿cuándo?, ¿cuánto?, ¿dónde?, ¿porqué?, ¿qué?, ¿quién? take the acute when used interrogatively; otherwise no accent is required.

Accent differentiates the meaning of the following: *dé* ('may give', *de* 'of'), *él* ('he', *el* 'the'), *más* ('more', *mas* 'but'), *mí* ('me', *mi* 'my'), *sí* ('self', 'yes', *si* 'if'), *sólo* ('only', *solo* 'alone').

Division of words

A consonant between two vowels and the second of two consonants must be taken over to the next line. But note carefully the following rules.

ch, *ll*, and *rr* are indivisible because they represent single sounds, and must be taken over: mu-chacho, arti-llería, pe-rro. *n* with tilde (*ñ* = *gn* in 'cognac') must be treated as a single consonant and therefore taken over in division: ca-ñón.

Consonants, except *s*, followed by *l* or *r* must be taken over with *l* or *r* undivided, but an exception is *tl* after initial *a*. Examples: ha-blar, a-flictivo, a-planar, a-prender, a-trio; but is-lámico, Is-raelítico, At-lántico.

Exactly contrary to the Latin rule, *s-t*, *s-p* must be divided: Es-teban, es-trella; ins-tar, ins-piración.

Divide compounds into their component parts: des-hacer, sub-lunar.

Diphthongs must never be divided.

Orthography

Note especially the common use of the single consonants *s*, *l*, *n*, *c* in such words as: disipa, óseo, ilegal, inocente, ocultar, necesario. But print *nn* in innovación, innumerable, and *cc* in acceso, acción.

Note also the dissimilation of *nm* in conmemoración, inmediatamente, inmenso, inmortal, etc. In Spanish print: aceptación, acomodación, asimilación, subrogar, sugestión, sujeto, suplicio.

Hard *g* before *e* or *i* is indicated by the insertion of *u*: guerrilla, guitarra.

Punctuation

Punctuation marks are similar to those used in English, but note that the exclamation (!) and the question (?) marks are inserted both before (inverted) and after the word or phrase, e.g. ¡Vé! ¿Dónde?

Quotation marks

Quotations are indicated by guillemets: dialogue by em rules (set close up); but when an author prefers the English style, his instructions are to be followed, and the compositor should be guided by the directions given with the work.

BIBLIOGRAPHY

THIS list is not exhaustive, but is a selection designed to provide a fairly comprehensive and reliable guide. A number of authorities are cited throughout this book, particularly in the sections dealing with foreign languages. They are not given again here.

Authors' and Printers' Dictionary, F. Howard Collins. 10th edition, Oxford University Press.

The Division of Words in Foreign Languages (French, German, Italian, Spanish). The Monotype Corporation Ltd.

British Standards Institution:
    Proof Correction and Copy Preparation. B.S. 1219.
    Bibliographical References. B.S. 1629.
    Alphabetical Arrangement. B.S. 1749.
    Letter Symbols, Signs and Abbreviations. B.S. 1991.
    Type-face Nomenclature. B.S. 2961.
    Transliteration of Cyrillic and Greek Characters. B.S. 2979.

Introduction to Typography, Oliver Simon. Faber & Faber Ltd.; revised edition, Penguin Books Ltd.

Methods of Book Design, Hugh Williamson. Oxford University Press.

A Manual of Style. University of Chicago Press.

Style for Print, R. A. Hewitt. Blandford Press Ltd.

The Printing of Mathematics, T. W. Chaundy, P. R. Barrett, Charles Batey. Oxford University Press.

Handbook for Chemical Society Authors. Special Publication No. 14, The Chemical Society.

INDEX

NOTES

NOTES

PRINTED IN GREAT BRITAIN
AT THE UNIVERSITY PRESS, OXFORD
BY VIVIAN RIDLER
PRINTER TO THE UNIVERSITY